directions

new FOR CONTINUING EDUCATION

number 1 • 1979

new directions for continuing education

a quarterly sourcebook
Alan B. Knox, Editor-in-Chief

number 1, 1979

enhancing proficiencies of continuing educators

alan b. knox
editor

Jossey-Bass Inc., Publishers
San Francisco • Washington • London

ENHANCING PROFICIENCIES OF CONTINUING EDUCATORS
New Directions for Continuing Education
Number 1, 1979
    Alan B. Knox, Editor

Copyright © 1979 by Jossey-Bass Inc., Publishers
              and
        Jossey-Bass Limited

Copyright under International, Pan American, and Universal Copyright Conventions. All rights reserved. No part of this issue may be reproduced in any form — except for brief quotation (not to exceed 500 words) in a review or professional work — without permission in writing from the publishers.

New Directions for Continuing Education is published quarterly by Jossey-Bass Inc., Publishers. Subscriptions are available at the regular rate for institutions, libraries, and agencies of $25 for one year. Individuals may subscribe at the special professional rate of $15 for one year. Application to mail at second-class postage rates is pending at San Francisco, California, and at additional mailing offices.

Correspondence:
Subscriptions, single-issue orders, change of address notices, undelivered copies, and other correspondence should be sent to *New Directions* Subscriptions, Jossey-Bass Inc., Publishers, 433 California Street, San Francisco, California 94104.
Editorial correspondence should be sent to the Editor-in-Chief, Alan B. Knox, Office for the Study of Continuing Professional Education, University of Illinois at Urbana–Champaign, Urbana, Illinois 61801.

Library of Congress Catalogue Card Number LC 78-73903

Cover design by Willi Baum
Manufactured in the United States of America

contents

editor's notes *alan b. knox* vii

overview: an introduction to the field 1
This sourcebook provides an overview of major areas of proficiency which contribute to the effectiveness of continuing education practitioners. It also suggests ways to acquire such proficiencies through personal efforts and through participation in professional development activities sponsored by agencies, associations, and universities.

practitioner proficiency 9
All categories of practitioners would benefit from three areas of proficiency—a perspective on the field (types of providers, relations with the parent organization, societal influences, resource identification), an understanding of adult development and learning, and certain personal qualities (such as commitment to lifelong learning, interpersonal effectiveness, and an innovative approach to practice).

administrators 23
Effective administrators demonstrate three areas of proficiency—administration (participation, resources, staffing, leadership), program development (needs, context, objectives, activities, evaluation), and planning and use of research.

teachers and counselors 43
Resource persons who help adults learn are more effective if they are knowledgeable about subject matter and adult development and are capable in the use of program development procedures (needs, context, objectives, activities, and evaluation).

policy makers 59
Policy makers include all those who make rules and allocate resources that affect the continuing education agency. A major area of proficiency for them is an understanding of desirable directions for agency development.

summary and future directions 67
Desirable future directions for action, policy, and research are proposed for the main areas of proficiency covered in the preceding chapters.

references 79

index 93

editor's notes

This sourcebook is the first issue of a new quarterly series on *New Directions for Continuing Education*. As such it defines the scope of the field of continuing education with which the series will deal. The main purpose of this sourcebook is to specify important areas of practitioner proficiency, and to suggest ways to acquire them through personal efforts and participation in professional development activities. The sourcebook focuses on three categories of practitioners—administrators, teachers, and policy makers—who are the intended readership.

This overview of continuing education practitioner proficiency can be useful in several ways, including: identification of major capabilities for practitioners to consider as they strive to become more effective; criteria for staff selection; suggestion of major topics as agencies, associations, and university graduate programs provide educational programs for continuing education practitioners; and generation of questions for research regarding continuing education practitioner proficiency.

Chapter One notes the recent trends that make specification of pracitioner proficiencies timely, discusses problems in the specification of core proficiencies, and describes ways in which practitioners can develop and use major areas of proficiency. Chapter Two describes three broad areas of proficiency that are important for all categories of practitioners, and presents illustrative concepts and generalizations for each. The three areas deal with a comprehensive perspective on the field, an understanding of adults as learners, and personal qualities such as interpersonal effectiveness; and a commitment to lifelong learning.

Chapters Three, Four, and Five deal similarly with major areas of proficiency for administrators, teachers and counselors, and policy makers. For administrators, the areas include administration, program development, and research. For teachers and counselors, the areas include knowledgeability regarding content and capability regarding the process of helping adults learn. For policy makers, the main proficiency is an understanding of desirable directions for agency development. In Chapters Four and Five attention is also given to ways in which administrators can help resource persons and policy makers become more proficient.

Chapter Six provides a summary and suggestions regarding desirable future directions for action, policy, and research related to continuing education practitioner proficiency. The citations of references in Chapter Six constitute a basic reading list of professional literature on continuing education of adults. Throughout the sourcebook, citations to the bibliography enable practitioners to engage in further reading related to each section of the sourcebook.

Hopefully, research and experience on this topic in the coming years will contribute to greater practitioner proficiency and program impact. Subsequent sourcebooks will be devoted to specific problems and opportunities that confront continuing education practitioners in their effort to identify relevant knowledge, exemplary practices, and desirable future directions.

Alan B. Knox
Editor

Alan B. Knox is professor of continuing education and director of the Office for the Study of Continuing Professional Education, University of Illinois at Urbana–Champaign. During more than twenty-five years he has taught in and administered a wide variety of educational programs for adults. Between 1973 and 1977 he served as Associate Vice Chancellor for Academic Affairs and Director of Continuing Education and Public Service for the University of Illinois at Urbana–Champaign. He has been a professor of adult and continuing education at the University of Nebraska at Lincoln, Teachers College Columbia University, and the University of Illinois at Urbana–Champaign, and during 1975–77 was chairman of the AEA Commission of Professors of Adult Education. An active researcher, he has authored more than sixty books, monographs, chapters, and articles on continuing education of adults.

It has become increasingly important that continuing education practitioners understand major areas of proficiency which contribute to their effectiveness, along with ways to acquire and use such proficiencies.

overview: an introduction to the field

In a well-known fairytale the miller's daughter tried to turn straw into gold, but was unable to do so without the contribution of Rumpelstiltskin. To succeed she had to solve the mystery of Rumpelstiltskin's name. After failing by use of trial and error, she was able to do so by use of a deliberate strategy. The object lesson of this familiar tale is suggestive of the contribution that professional proficiency makes to the effectiveness of continuing education practitioners.

Administrators and teachers pursue the golden goal of helping adults learn, adapt, grow, and achieve greater fulfillment. In doing so they use resources that are of value but as common as straw—ideas, books, meeting rooms, and experts. Many find, however, that this alchemy is difficult to accomplish. Those who are successful have discovered that the mystery ingredient is professional proficiency and that trial and error is unlikely to solve the mystery. Success goes to those who develop a deliberate strategy for increasing their proficiency.

In the fairytale, the deliberate strategy that succeeded after trial and error failed consisted of a broad and active search for information relevant to the problem—benefited by serendipity when a courier overheard an old man's curious chant whose last line was "and Rumpelstiltskin is my name." In real life, many continuing education administrators and teachers who are unaware of useful concepts and practices in the field engage in trial and error as they seek to "turn straw into gold."

This sourcebook is designed to facilitate the "search for Rumpelstiltskin" by identifying major areas of proficiency that effective practitioners weave into their deliberate strategies to help adults learn.

Perhaps the primary challenge of the coming decade in continuing education of adults revolves around defining and increasing the professional proficiency of workers in the field. These include administrators, teachers, counselors, and policy makers. Such practitioners work in various segments of the field, which reflect the type of parent organization of which continuing education agencies are a part. Included are educational institutions such as schools, community colleges, universities, and a wide variety of other organizations such as labor unions, the military, religious institutions, professional associations, hospitals, libraries, museums, voluntary associations, and employers as providers of continuing education. The organizational unit concerned with the continuing education function typically provides educational programs for adults who participate on a part time or short term basis.

Many continuing education practitioners have entered the field only recently and lack a clear understanding of major areas of proficiency that could contribute to their effectiveness. This is apparent when a recent practitioner painstakingly develops a procedure that has already been widespread in the field for years, when a practitioner is uncertain where to begin familiarizing himself with relevant professional literature, and when the program committee of an association of continuing education practitioners has difficulty identifying important and relevant topics for an annual meeting.

Continuing education practitioners would benefit from an understanding of the field of continuing education, an understanding of adults as learners, and personal qualities such as interpersonal effectiveness. Effective administrators are proficient regarding administration, program development, and research. Effective teachers and counselors are knowledgeable about subject matter content and are able to help adults learn. Effective policy makers understand desirable directions for agency development. This sourcebook provides an overview of these capabilities and how to develop and use them.

recent trends

After generations when the field of adult and continuing education was marginal and virtually invisible, concepts and practices of lifelong learning during adulthood are becoming part of the outlook of the general public and of practitioners in education of children and youth. References to adult learning are now commonplace in newspapers, television, and publications in all professional fields. As a result, many people are now beginning to plan and conduct continuing education activities. Some of them are challenging the sense of franchise that many long-time practitioners enjoyed during the earlier era of benign neglect.

During the past decade or so, public expectations of adult education have soared. This optimism is reflected in legislation and in favorable articles in the popular press. Combined with the explosive increase in the size and visibility of the field, such rising expectations have produced the current challenge to continuing education practitioners. Will they be able to achieve the new expectations?

purpose of sourcebook

This initial sourcebook of a new quarterly series, *New Directions for Continuing Education,* deals with continuing education practitioner proficiency. Its purpose is to specify important areas of such proficiency and to suggest ways to expand them through personal efforts, and through participation in professional development activities provided by agencies, associations, and universities. In addition, this initial sourcebook helps define the scope of the field of continuing education with which the new series will deal. The references cited throughout the volume refer to the literature available to practitioners who want to increase their proficiency.

The field of continuing education depends on contributions by many categories of people, such as adult learners, teachers, counselors, support personnel, program administrators, directors, representatives of co-sponsors, administrators of parent organizations, policy makers, researchers, and professors. This initial sourcebook focuses on skills needed by three categories of personnel—administrators, teachers, and policy makers—who are the intended readership. It includes abilities important for all practitioners as well as those that are distinctive for each. It does not include some additional aspects, such as command of research procedures, which are needed by researchers and professors.

This statement on practitioner proficiencies builds on many previous statements on the topic (Aker, 1963; Apps, 1972; Blakely, 1966; Boyd, 1969; Bunch, 1968; Campbell, 1977; Chamberlain, 1961; Copeland, 1973; Essert, 1960; Griffith and Cloutier, 1972, 1974; Houle, 1956, 1964, 1970; Hoyt, 1969; Ingham and Qazilbash, 1968; Knowles, 1962; Knox, 1973; Kreitlow, 1956, 1965; Long and Agyekum, 1974; Madry, 1963; Noel and Parsons, 1973; Price, 1960; Robinson, 1962; Rossman and Bunning, 1978; Scates, 1963; Spear, 1976; Thomas, 1963; Tough, 1968a; Veri, 1968, nd; Verner and others, 1970; White, 1956). Many of these earlier statements were oriented toward graduate study with a major in adult and continuing education, and emphasized course topics deemed important. This statement deals with proficiencies important for all practitioners in the field regardless of preparation and background.

Listed below are some ways in which continuing education practitioners might use this overview of areas of important professional proficiencies.

1. An *individual practitioner* interested in becoming more effective might compare relevant sections of the overview with an assessment of his or her own current proficiency to identify desirable areas of *professional growth.*

2. A *continuing education director interested in recruitment* and selection of a program administrator for the agency might use the areas of proficiency important for all practitioners and for administrators in the preparation of a *position description,* of *selection criteria,* and of *orientation experiences.*

3. A *continuing education program administrator* interested in selection and orientation of *resource persons* to help plan and conduct continuing education courses or workshops might use the areas of proficiency important

for all practitioners, and for teachers and counselors to select and work with them so that they become more effective in helping adults learn.

4. A *continuing education agency staff member* with responsibility for conducting *staff development activities* for agency administrators and resource persons might use relevant sections of the overview to identify *important topics* for staff development activities.

5. A *continuing education practitioner* who helps *plan meetings and workshops* for continuing education professional associations might use relevant sections of the overview as a source of ideas for a survey of members to identify *attractive themes and session topics.*

6. A *continuing education director* interested in improving the *policy making* that affects the agency might use the areas of proficiency important for all practitioners and for policy makers to *decide on the concepts* to convey to such policy makers when occasions arise and to select effective ways to do so.

7. A *professor of adult and continuing education* might compare relevant sections of the overview with *graduate program* courses and internships to identify adjustments that might be made in course offerings or topic emphases within courses in an effort to prepare capable practitioners for the field.

8. A *continuing education researcher* might use the overview to generate questions for research to *validate and extend generalizations* about continuing education practitioner proficiency.

proficiency

In this sourcebook, the concept of proficiency is related to both knowledge and action. The term *professional proficiency* refers to a desirable level that most of the highly effective practitioners would be expected to achieve. The dictionary definition of proficiency emphasizes high levels of competence, adeptness, and confident control, based on expertise, skill, and knowledge acquired through education and experience. A proficient person has the capability and reserve power to *perform well* in a specific situation and to meet the demands or requirements of a situation or work demand. This contrasts with a person who may have formal qualifications, or may even hold a position in the field, but who is *not able to perform well.* The term "proficiency" also contrasts with that of "competence" which emphasizes minimum, satisfactory, or moderate levels of capability.

The concept of proficiency links understanding and performance. A practitioner's knowledge regarding goals and procedures in the field contributes to proficiency, but must be combined with understanding and experience in actual tasks and roles to produce it. Professional performance consists of what practitioners actually do when they deal with problems and opportunities in which the situation may prevent them from using the proficiency they possess. By contrast, proficiency consists of what they can do when given the opportunity.

Closely related to actual proficiency and performance is the individual's sense of being proficient and competent. It is the result of success; it also influences the tasks an individual undertakes. The new program administrator who successfully coordinates several conferences begins to develop this sense of proficiency. The sense of proficiency or competence is an important ingredient of personality development throughout life (White, 1961, 1963, 1972).

Creative problem solving, combining theory and practice, enables practitioners to learn from everyday experiences and to relate insights from the sciences and humanities, along with professional knowledge, tacit understanding, and appreciation of events in the course of their professional practice (Adelson, 1976; Bunge, 1973; Carter, 1968; Glaser, 1976; Gross and Osterman, 1972; Jantsch, 1975; Mager and Pipe, 1972; Miller, Galanter, and Pribram, 1960; Newell and Simon, 1972; Ruesch, 1975; Simon, 1969).

In contrast with scholarship in the sciences and humanities in which specialization is rewarded, in professional practice generally, the ability to integrate concepts and procedures from diverse sources to accomplish tasks is an important capability. This is implicit when continuing education practitioners refer to themselves as generalists. Their tasks tend to cluster around the program development process and agency functioning.

Core Proficiencies of All Practitioners. For continuing education practitioners, the issue of specialized versus core proficiencies revolves around the types of provider agencies in which they work, and around their professional roles. Frequently mentioned core proficiencies are related to educational goals for adults, adult development and learning, program development procedures, and general agency functioning (Leagans, Copeland, and Kaiser, 1971). Specific procedures and terminology related to a specific type of agency or role such as administrator, teacher, or counselor tend to vary greatly from situation to situation (Noel and Parsons, 1973). Efforts to increase proficiency can deal with a widely shared core of concepts and procedures which requires individualization and specialization so that workers can perceive its relevance and application to their own needs (Copeland, 1973). These core proficiencies have emerged in the findings from most previous efforts (Aker, 1963; Campbell, 1977; Chamberlain, 1961; Scates, 1963; Spear, 1976; Veri, 1968; Verner and others, 1970; T. White, 1956).

Problems of Specification. An analysis of professional proficiency for continuing education practitioners can benefit from a perusal of the literature on mastery learning and competency-based education which surfaced in preparatory education during this decade. It should be kept in mind that the central issue in competency-based preparatory education has been a curricular and instructional overemphasis on the theory of the subject matter and a lack of relevance to adult life roles. This issue seems to be less severe in continuing education of adults generally, where relevance has been emphasized, and in efforts to increase the proficiency of continuing education practitioners in particular, where action and results have been emphasized. As Dewey (1929) noted a half century ago, the seeming conflict between content and roles can be somewhat resolved by emphasizing as a major goal of education the development of intelligence as a method of action.

The essence of competency-based preparatory education is that most students should acquire basic mastery in influencing their environment and thus acquire both efficacy and self-confidence. The achievement of educational objectives relevant to adult role performance is the goal, and types of learning activities and time required to achieve mastery are variable means to achieve the goal. Although some attention is given to student goal pursuits, the main source of objectives tends to be role expectations (Block, 1978; Davies, 1973; Hall and Jones, 1976; *Phi Delta Kappan,* 1978; Spady, 1977; Spady and Mitchell, 1977; Torshen, 1977; Trivett, 1975). The term *competency-based education* is somewhat confounded by its popular application to remedial programs for youths who were not meeting the requirements for high school graduation. This focus on minimum achievement is inadequate for the specification of optimum proficiency by continuing education practitioners.

Some of the problems that have been identified in relation to competency-based preparatory education can serve as cautions for those who seek to help continuing education practitioners acquire professional proficiency (Griffith and Cervero, 1977). Most of the problems are difficulties regarding specification and emphasis (Block, 1978; Broudy, 1972; Eisner, 1967, 1969; Kemmis and Stake, 1974). For example, which competencies that young students could master are most important in relation to adult role performance? How can adequate balance be maintained for the affective domain, in light of greater ease in specification of behavioral objectives related to knowledge and skills? Or, fundamentally, how can behavioral outcomes be specified with sufficient precision to be able to establish minimum competence? It is also difficult to judge the value of the educational objectives, as well as the extent to which they are achieved. In addition, effective instructional strategies must be selected and used so that most learners will in fact become competent.

In the assessment of competency-based education, it seems desirable to go beyond mastery of learning tasks so as to foster the desire for further learning and its application. In continuing education (such as in the Cooperative Extension Service and in training programs employers conduct for employees) a major criterion of program success is the extent to which practices are changed. Especially in efforts to increase the professional proficiency of continuing education practitioners, their impact on the provider agency and on the adult clients is the major criterion against which to validate the effectiveness of in-service education programs.

developing proficiency

Concepts of professional proficiency in continuing education can be useful in several ways. Individual practitioners and their instructors can use them to help establish professional development objectives. General concepts from the literature can sensitize them to aspects of performance likely to be crucial to success (Swanson and Carter, 1967). Recognition of important areas of proficiency should help practitioners identify and understand unsatisfactory performance (Miller, 1977; Schein, 1978). This can occur through the understanding of areas of proficiency both as goals or standards against which to judge performance, and as criteria against which to diagnose unsatisfactory aspects of performance (Veri, 1968).

Efforts by continuing education practitioners to increase their own proficiency can be highly self-directed (Veri, 1968). Certainly this seems appropriate for practitioners engaged in helping other adults learn. A listing of important areas of competence can be used to alert practitioners to those deserving particular attention (Knox, 1974), to prepare competency-based learning packages (Murray, 1976), and to identify those aspects of experience instrumental in the purposeful and systematic efforts to "learn from experience" (Blake and Mouton, 1976).

Concepts about proficiencies of continuing education practitioners are frequently the concern of the professional development activities provided by agencies, associations, and universities. For example, competency-based learning packages can be used in in-service programs for practitioners conducted by each of these providers. Lists of important areas of professional proficiency can also be used to select topics for workshops: Continuing education agencies (such as a public school adult education division, the Cooperative Extension Service in a state, or an industrial training department) can create committees to plan in-service education activities for those who plan and conduct their continuing education programs; national professional associations (such as the Adult Education Association, the National University Extension Association, or the National Association for Public Continuing and Adult Education) can conduct special workshops and presessions for members, in addition to planning the regular annual national, regional, and state conferences. Finally, university graduate programs in adult and continuing education can conduct workshops in addition to offering degree credit courses, both on and off campus, which focus on these proficiencies. In each of these instances, an individual or a committee decides on topics for increasing proficiency. Identification of important areas of practitioner proficiency can help these providers select high priority topics and to develop learning activities likely to have an impact on practice.

Currently, about eighty universities in North America have graduate programs at the master's and/or doctoral level with a specialization in adult, continuing, or extension education. During the past two decades there have been repeated efforts to identify important areas of proficiency which such graduate programs should seek to develop (Aker, 1963; Campbell, 1977; Chamberlain, 1961; Douglah and Moss, 1969; Ingham and Qazilbash, 1968; Ingham and Robbins, 1977; Knox, 1973; Kreitlow, 1965; Scates, 1963; Veri, 1968; Verner and others, 1970). Broader conceptualizations of important practitioner proficiencies can improve such graduate programs. Although many past efforts to identify practitioner proficiencies dealt with students or graduates of graduate programs, this has not always been the case. There have been studies focusing on adult basic education (ABE) teachers and on Cooperative Extension Service (CES) county extension advisers. In this sourcebook, an effort has been made to include papers on workers in the field as well as those in graduate study in adult, continuing, or extension education.

Policy makers concerned with lifelong learning can use ability concepts to help clarify the scope and major emphases within the field. Researchers can use and refine such concepts and analyze the relative importance of various proficiencies in effective performance.

summary

Many continuing education practitioners lack an understanding of major areas of desirable professional proficiency, although they could be useful in becoming more effective. This sourcebook focuses on three categories of personnel—administrators, resource persons, and policy makers—who are the intended readership. Although proficiencies are difficult to specify, an understanding of their major areas can be used to select effective staff members, to focus self-directed study efforts, and to plan in-service education activities for practitioners.

Subsequent chapters of this sourcebook describe major areas of professional proficiency that seem important for all categories of practitioners (except researchers and professors) along with distinctive areas of proficiency that seem to be especially important for administrators, for teachers and counselors, and for policy makers. The concluding chapter contains highlights from the preceding chapters and suggests promising future directions.

Some areas of proficiency (such as a perspective on the field, an understanding of adults as learners, and certain personal qualities) are important for all continuing education practitioners.

practitioner proficiency

All categories of practitioners engaged in continuing education would appear to benefit from three broad areas of proficiency (Campbell, 1977; ERIC/AE, 1970; Hansen, Klink, and Kramer, 1973; Rossman and Bunning, 1978; Spear, 1976; Veri, 1968; Verner and others, 1970). Two are mainly cognitive—an understanding of the field of continuing education and an understanding of adults as learners. The third is mainly affective, and consists of personal qualities such as positive attitudes toward lifelong learning, effective interpersonal relations, and innovativeness. The ways in which these three areas of proficiency are acquired and employed by administrators, by teachers and counselors, and by policy makers vary considerably, but each area of proficiency seems to be important to practitioner effectiveness. This chapter briefly describes each area of shared proficiency, provides a rationale for its importance, and suggests its contribution to goal setting as well as personnel selection and development. Illustrative generalizations and references for further reading are also included.

perspective on the field

Each profession socializes its members into the field so that they share understandings and commitments. This process is doubly difficult for the field of continuing education of adults. The fragmentation of the field and "part-timeness" of many agency staff members make it difficult for practitioners to gain a comprehensive perspective on scope, trends, and issues. In addition, practitioners enter the field from varied backgrounds and, unlike practitioners in most professions, do not share common preparatory professional education experiences or even membership in a common professional association. However, many of the most effective continuing education practitioners do achieve a perspective on the field, including an understanding of providers of programs, relations with parent organizations, societal influences, and awareness of resources. Except for the few practitioners who complete courses about continuing education, most of this overall picture of the field and its basic definitions tends to be acquired through an informal socialization process. Most of the generalizations about the field are based on descriptive professional literature. Little research has been conducted to analyze either the major concepts of the field, or the contribution that an understanding of the field makes to professional effectiveness of practitioners. However, writers about the field repeatedly refer to how important it is that practitioners have a perspective on scope, trends, and issues (Chamberlain, 1961; Houle, 1957; Jensen, Liveright, and Hallenbeck, 1964; Knox, 1974; Smith, Aker, and Kidd, 1970).

Types of Providers

The coherence of the field stems from the common function of helping adults learn. The fragmentation of the field stems from the wide variety of agencies that do so. Most efforts to define the scope and structure of the field focus on the categories of provider agencies (Knowles, 1977). The distinction is usually made between those continuing education agencies which are parts of educational institutions (schools, community colleges, universities) having educational resources (teachers, books, facilities) and seeking participants, and those which are parts of all types of other organizations (employers, labor unions, religious institutions, associations) and have members who need increased proficiency and seek educational resources. Practitioners with even a year's experience in the field typically gain some understanding of their provider agency and perhaps some perspective on others with the same type of parent organization. They learn to recognize alternatives and to learn from the experience of others. Similar benefits regarding sharing and innovation can result from familiarity with agencies and practitioners from other segments of this broad field.

There are several ways in which practitioners can acquire increased understanding of various types of provider agencies and their programs, goals, and procedures. Included are visits to other agencies, participation in association meetings and activities that include practitioners from other types of agencies, and reading of books, journals, and newsletters that deal with issues and programs from various segments of the field. The resulting understanding of how the field of continuing education functions can enable practitioners to discover innovative practices that can be adapted to their own agencies, to consider the relative importance of various agency and program goals within the field, and to explore collaborative relationships among agencies that take into account both similarities and differences.

Parent Organization

Most continuing education agencies are dependent units of parent organizations whose main purpose is other than continuing education of adults on a part or short term basis. For example, the main purpose of a business in which an education and training department is located is to produce goods and services, and the main purpose of a school system in which an adult education division is located is to educate children and youth who typically attend full time. Most experienced practitioners recognize that relationships between the continuing education agency and the rest of the parent organization greatly affect agency performance (Knox, 1975). This is especially so for agency directors who deal with policy, staffing, and resource allocation.

An understanding of the purposes and procedures of the parent organization, along with dynamics of organizational stability and change, can enable continuing education practitioners to function as valued members of the total parent organization as well as to serve as effective advocates for the continuing education agency. Although the research and procedural literature on organizational behavior can be useful to practitioners in this regard, the crucial ingredient is experience with and reflection about relationships between one's own agency and the rest of the parent organization of which it is a part. In addition to an understanding of organizational dynamics, effective interaction with members of the parent organization provides the basis for using such understandings to advance the continuing education function. An understanding of agency functioning also enables practitioners to use an awareness of societal trends and issues to formulate agency initiatives in light of parent organization purposes.

Societal Influences

Over the years, continuing education agencies have been greatly influenced by their societal context. Within the agency's service area, community problems (such as employment, health), available resources (such as participants, resource persons), national and international trends (such as federal funding for adult basic education or for continuing education for the health professions), and the offerings of other providers can have a major and sometimes sudden impact on program size and emphasis. An understanding of societal trends and issues is especially important for continuing education practitioners if they are to do more than react to societal influences. Such understanding can allow early recognition of emerging trends, identification of implications for the agency, and initiation of continuing education programs with goals and procedures that harness or perhaps deflect societal influences.

It is very difficult to fully understand many societal influences and their implications for continuing education through direct personal experience alone. Therefore a subtle but important quality of practitioners with a sense of direction is a broad perspective on trends and issues based on familiarity with the literature on the history of the field (Grattan, 1955, 1971; Knowles, 1977), recurrent policy issues (Blakely and Lappin, 1969; Knowles, 1977), social change (Bennis and others, 1976), community power structure, recent legislation, as well as emerging issues for topics on which continuing education programs are focused. Practitioners who read about continuing education trends and major social problems are more likely to recognize emerging issues to which their agency can respond effectively than those who attend solely to daily operational concerns. Attention to goals and priorities can also be heightened by some analysis of how continuing education functions in other national settings (Grattan, 1955, 1971). Comparative analysis helps practitioners recognize strategic factors in their own situation. Participation in professional association activities can enable them to compare their own assessments of trends, issues, and responses with the assessments of colleagues elsewhere in order to test and refine their own sense of direction. This sense of the developing future is a great asset to continuing education practitioners, but it is a capacity that requires reflection on the meanings of events.

Resource Identification

Another benefit of having a broad perspective on the field is an awareness of resources which other practitioners might overlook. Some resources are in the form of professional literature, discussing concepts which might be useful (for example) in developing a rationale for investment in continuing education. Awareness of the basic literature in general, such as the references cited in Chapter Six of this sourcebook, might be useful. Other resources might include people who could contribute to program planning or implementation. For example, awareness of people from state agencies can be helpful for some programs. Still other resources are fiscal, such as funds to support special projects if only a practitioner knew how to prepare successful proposals to obtain them. Practitioner proficiency regarding acquisition of resources includes both awareness of sources and effective strategies for obtaining them. Inventories of resources can alert practitioners to sources. A related proficiency is the ability to produce such inventories when they do not exist. Especially for human and fiscal resources, experience is a valuable ingredient in the acquisition of increased ability in planning and implementing strategies for obtaining resources. Participation in a professional association can introduce a practitioner to valuable colleagues who work in other segments of the field. A practitioner's proficiency regarding awareness of resources is reflected in the breadth of vision and persuasiveness of a proposal rationale, in the attraction of fresh new talent to an agency, and in the identification of appropriate but underutilized funding sources.

The importance and application of professional proficiency regarding awareness of resources can be illustrated by the process of preparing a proposal for an external grant. Many practitioners want to conduct continuing education programs which have high priority in the agency but cannot be conducted without special financial support. Such support is available from a wide variety of philanthropic foundations and governmental granting agencies. The practitioner's task is to match needs and resources, and this is aided by an awareness of relevant resources and a strategy for proposal preparation. Information about relevant resources is available from various sources. Included are general directories of resources in the field of continuing education (Niemi and Jessen, 1976), the *Foundation Directory* (1960, 1977), periodic announcements of new grant programs and requests for proposals in publications such as the *Federal Register,* and even a library reference department. Some practitioners have a card file on outstanding resource persons they would like to use when the occasion arises.

A practitioner is more likely to identify and obtain needed resources if an effective strategy for proposal preparation is used. Such a strategy typically includes development of a clear and persuasive rationale regarding needs, objectives, and appropriateness of procedures. This rationale contributes to the identification of likely funding sources and other pertinent resources, and enhances the persuasiveness of the proposal that is submitted.

Practitioners can acquire a greater awareness of resources in various ways. Included are reviewing directories and other listings of resources, discussing strategies with practitioners who successfully obtain grants and specialized resources, and preparing project proposals. Publications such as the *Chronicle of Higher Education* report the types of projects currently being supported by funding agencies.

adults as learners

A second broad area of professional proficiency, and one that is shared with practitioners in all of the helping professions who work with adults, is an understanding of adult development and learning. The generalizations in this section illustrate the understanding of adults as learners typical of effective practitioners. The growth and increased effectiveness of adult participants is the purpose of most continuing education activities. The voluntariness of most continuing education programs makes it especially important that offerings be responsive to client needs and interests in order to attract and retain participants. Thus, an understanding of adults as learners is of critical importance to teachers, counselors, administrators, and policy makers as they make decisions about program purposes and procedures. An understanding of adults as learners includes attention to reasons for participation in educative activities and to the dynamics of learning. It also includes attention to self-directed participation in informal learning projects in which almost all adults engage (Tough, 1968b, 1971, 1978), as well as in agency-provided continuing education activities with which most practitioners are mainly concerned. Both formal and informal purposeful and systematic learning activities typically occur on a part or short term basis concurrent with adult life roles to which the continuing education program usually relates. Because adult learners seek to apply what they learn to current role performance, a detailed understanding of adult development and learning is of great importance for all types of practitioners (Knox, 1977a).

Adult Development

There are many aspects of adult development that have implications for continuing education practitioners, such as expectations and performance in family, occupation, and community roles throughout adult life. In addition to adult role performance and influences from the societal context in which it occurs, the professional literature on adult development includes generalizations about developmental trends and mechanisms regarding physical condition, health, and personality. Continuing education practitioners tend to be especially interested in interactions among the foregoing generalizations that help to predict and explain successful participation in educative activity. Such generalizations help to explain both the decision to participate and the extent of application of new learnings.

The increase in tested knowledge from research about adult development during recent decades enables practitioners to move beyond a generalized commitment to adult participants and to apply detailed insight into developmental mechanisms and adaptation of adults. Those practitioners who do acquire such detailed insights and research based generalizations, do so mainly through reading the professional literature on adult development (Knox, 1977a). However, such organized knowledge can be greatly augmented through perceptiveness and reflectiveness in daily interactions with individual adults, and it is in this arena that organized knowledge about adult development must be applied if it is to be most useful to practitioners.

The generalizations in this section illustrate the many and detailed generalizations about adult development that can be part of practitioner proficiencies in their efforts to plan and conduct responsive educational programs. Continuing education participation is an aspect of adult life of special interest to practitioners. Such participation declines somewhat with age but increases greatly with educational level. This reflects a relationship between educational level and adult information seeking. Adults with little formal education seldom engage in instrumental information seeking from print and electronic media or from impersonal experts, but instead rely mainly on conversations with family and friends. This has implications for the nature of the efforts to attract participants and of the educational materials likely to communicate effectively with the target audience.

Adult life cycle trends in performance of family, occupational, and community roles suggest ways in which continuing education participation might facilitate adaptation and growth related to each role area. Regarding family role: As adolescents leave home, parents lose satisfaction from active parenting but gain freedom to pursue personal interests. Regarding occupational role: Young workers tend to excel in tasks that use speed, strength, memory, and production of novel solutions, in contrast with older workers who tend to excel in tasks that use experience, steadiness, attendance, patience, and conscientiousness. Regarding community roles in recreation, organizations, political affairs, and religious organizations: Although extent of social participation is stable during most of adulthood, the mix of types of activities shifts from active in young adulthood to interpersonal in middle age to introspective in old age.

From time to time the stability of adulthood is punctuated by role change events such as the birth of the first child, a move to another community, or retirement. Some adaptation is inescapable, but problems of adjustment can be moderated by satisfactory social participation and warm human relationships. Such change events typically produce heightened readiness to learn which, if recognized, can contribute to the effectiveness of marketing and instructional activities. Such major role changes can also be associated with personality development which continues throughout life. The impetus for change may come from the individual or from society, and constructive change is more likely when facilitated by both personal striving and societal encouragement. Both gradual trends and role changes contribute to adult life cycle shifts in values and interests. The outlook of many young adults is characterized by expansiveness and high expectations, in contrast with efforts toward self-limitation and reduction of frustration which are more widespread during middle age.

From adolescence through middle age, a person's self-concept tends to become more positive. Self-concept and performance interact. During adolescence many young people develop dreams of who they want to become which sometimes sustain them during the striving of young adulthood. During midlife reassessments, such abstract commitments tend to wane; in the process of becoming their own person many adults conclude that the future is now and the years remaining become more important than the years spent. Although being self-directed instead of dependent is part of the concept of maturity and adulthood, some adults are concerned about being too reactive. Self-directedness entails assertiveness and a sense of direction (Gould, 1978; Levinson, 1978; Vaillant, 1977). Many adults who participate in continuing education want to be self-directed in the learner role as well. Practitioners who understand such generalizations about adult development can appreciate the variability that occurs; they can help adults approach specific concerns and change events developmentally by recognizing options and opportunities for growth (Bolles, 1978).

Adult Learning

Generalizations about adult learning abilities and dynamics are especially important for those who help adults learn, but such generalizations are also useful for those who select, supervise, and evaluate instructional personnel and programs. Very experienced and effective teachers of adults tend to discover some basic generalizations about the conditions under which adults with various characteristics learn effectively. These generalizations relate to adjustment in the learning situation, search for meaning, learning ability, physiological influences, pacing, interference, reinforcement, and feedback. The scholarly literature on adult learning can help to enhance and accelerate the acquisition of such understandings (Howe, 1977; Knox, 1977a).

The following generalizations illustrate the variety of major concepts about adult learning which should be tools available to all practitioners as they themselves help adults to learn or assist others who do so. Effective practitioners typically understand that almost every adult is able to learn about almost any subject, given sufficient time and attention. Furthermore, adults vary in learning ability, but for the individual person, learning ability is quite stable during most of adulthood. Practitioners who gain this understanding solely from anecdotal experience working with adult learners can be optimistic and supportive when helping adults learn. However, practitioners who know the research findings upon which this generalization is based can be even more convinced and convincing, and can more effectively help participants achieve their full potential.

Learning is enhanced by satisfactory adjustment to the physical and social environment of the learning activity. A participant who feels estranged by social relationships or threatened by the educational expectations typically has difficulty learning and withdraws. Practitioners who understand this seek to create a setting for learning that helps them achieve important and relevant educational objectives, encourages them to feel welcome, provides reassurance to offset fear of failure, encourages group support and sharing, and provides freedom to explore within democratic limits the achievement of objectives and discovery of additional desirable objectives.

Most people perform well below their ceiling capacity. Furthermore, adults underestimate their learning ability by overemphasizing their early school experience and underemphasizing their recent informal learning experiences. Social class differences in verbal behavior further confound the situation. Practitioners who recognize this can provide newcomers with attractive learning tasks in which they will readily succeed so that they gain realistic estimates of their learning abilities. Evaluation feedback during learning activities can further contribute to effective learning.

Especially for older adults, learning can be affected by the interrelated influences of biological systems, mental health, nutrition, and exercise. After age fifty, vision and hearing decline gradually. An impoverished learning environment and disuse of study skills will also affect learning performance. Practitioners can minimize the extent to which these conditions hamper learning by suggesting corrective lenses or hearing aids when needed, and by providing satisfactory illumination, sound amplification, print sizes, exposure time, and combined audio and visual presentation. They can also emphasize learner abilities and minimize features related to disabilities by drawing upon learners' experience so that wisdom can be substituted for brilliance. Although these desirable features are well known, they are frequently disregarded.

Adults learn most effectively when they proceed at their own pace. With age, adults become more cautious in learning tasks; because they have more experience and information (some of which can interfere with the learning task), they have to engage in a wider search when trying to remember. The basic concepts (or cognitive structure) which an adult has about a topic can either help or hinder learning more about the topic. Practitioners can help adults learn by allowing for individualization and self-pacing; by use of advance organizers, review of prerequisite concepts, memory aids, and focus questions which diagnose current understanding and build more adequate cognitive structures to facilitate learning and recall. Memorable encounters, along with evaluation and recognition of individual achievement, also help adults proceed through learning tasks.

Effective adult learning is an active search for meaning. Adults seldom learn, remember, and use answers for which they do not already have the question. Practitioners who understand this point seek to involve participants actively in objective setting to increase relevance, in selection and organization of learning activities to fit a preferred learning style, and in evaluation to increase responsiveness and use of increased proficiency. The aim for a practitioner in attending to a participant's active concern with goals and procedures is to help adults learn how to learn (Smith, 1976; Smith and Haverkamp, 1977).

Practitioners who understand the foregoing generalizations about adult learning can use them to design effective learning activities, to select and supervise instructional personnel, and in the evaluation of learning activities to achieve program improvement.

For concepts about both adult development and adult learning, experience and reading tend to be the main ways in which proficiency is acquired. Experience with a variety of adults, especially in learning situations, can provide a practitioner with a holistic sense of the various ways in which adults function, including motivation and striving. This general perspective on adulthood gained from experience can generate some of the questions to which the literature on adult development and learning can provide answers. Another way for practitioners to increase their understanding of adult development and learning is to discuss specific learners or clients with other practitioners, similar to case reviews in the mental health field. In this process, practitioners who vary in their perspective on a client and their expertise regarding adult development and learning discuss a specific client in an effort to understand personal and situational aspects of the developmental process and to plan effective forms of assistance. Courses or workshops on adult development and learning can also be helpful.

Proficiency regarding adult development and learning provides a broadened perspective on developmental trends and processes, and on the dynamics of learning—which can sensitize a practitioner to important features of a specific client, target market, or learning group. The practitioner can then be more focused regarding educational needs, reasons for participation, or relevant instructional materials. An understanding of adult development and learning can also contribute to clientele analysis and priority setting.

personal qualities

The foregoing areas of proficiency—perspectives on the field and on adults as learners—have emerged from quite a few studies designed to identify important areas. Many of the specific concepts have emerged repeatedly, and a common sense fit seems to exist between an understanding of the field and of learners on the one hand and the effectiveness of practitioners on the other. By contrast, personal qualities, the third broad area of abilities, have far less support in the literature of the field (Campbell, 1977; Ingham and Hanks, 1978; Mocker, 1974). Three aspects of capability are subsumed under the heading of personal qualities. They are commitment, interpersonal effectiveness, and an innovative approach to practice.

Commitment

One of the most frequently mentioned personal qualities is a commitment to lifelong learning during adulthood. This value is reflected in a belief in the importance of adult learning and adaptation, in an optimism about the extent of learning and growth that can occur, in a commitment to continuing education activities to facilitate adult learning, and in the personal example that the practitioner sets as a lifelong learner. Although there is little research evidence that such personal values and beliefs are crucial to satisfactory performance as a continuing education practitioner, they are mentioned frequently as important; and a zest for learning by one's self and by other adults certainly seems desirable for practitioners for whom lifelong learning during adulthood is at the core of their professional activity.

It is unclear how people acquire a commitment to lifelong learning and to the broad field that facilitates the process (Pepper, 1958; Smith, 1976). It seems likely that personal zest for learning is acquired before entry into the field and is an influence on the decision to do so. It also seems likely that exposure to one or more effective and enthusiastic practitioners can evoke commitment to at least one segment of the field, and that contact with those in other segments can contribute to a comprehension of the field as a whole. In practice, many practitioners have dual allegiances—a primary allegiance to their own segment or type of parent organization and a secondary allegiance to the field at large.

Practitioners with a strong commitment to continuing education tend to be more enthusiastic about their work and to generate enthusiasm in others; to keep helping adults learn at the focus of their mission and to set priorities accordingly; and to emphasize cooperative effort and professionalism rather than competitiveness.

Interpersonal Effectiveness

Although personal commitment matters indeed, there is even greater evidence for the importance of getting along well with various adults for effective practice. Anecdotal evidence and beliefs within the field regarding the importance of interpersonal effectiveness are widespread.

Most practitioners accomplish what they do with and through other adults. Experienced policy makers know that useful policies make a constructive difference; this is aided greatly by effective relationships with those who implement them at the stages of both formulation and implementation. Administrators typically function in power poor positions in which lack of policy support causes them to provide a type of human cement that holds many continuing education agencies together. This along with delegation, supervision, coordination, and an ongoing concern for staffing and resource acquisition places a premium on effective interpersonal relations. The ability to win cooperation, especially from experts and those who control resources, is evinced repeatedly by the most effective practitioners. For example, an effective conference coordinator must work with many client groups who vary in their understanding of the prerequisites for successful programs, and with resource persons whose expertise must be respected and whose special contribution must be orchestrated. Efforts to win cooperation occur in planning committees and in individual contacts by phone, mail, and in person. A sense of direction, responsiveness, persuasiveness, and follow-through are contributory qualities.

The voluntariness of continuing education participation places a premium on effective interpersonal relations on the part of teachers and counselors. Concern and respect for adults with varied backgrounds, a sense of humor, and responsiveness and flexibility while helping adults learn are qualities that have emerged frequently as desirable characteristics (Knox and Farmer, 1977; Sagoff, 1965; Spear, 1976; Whipple, 1957). Establishing rapport and making participants feel welcome are procedures that are stressed especially during initial encounters. Policy makers need effective interpersonal relationships as they deal with the variety of people who contribute to policy formulation and those who implement it. This ability also contributes to productive interactions among members of a policy board or committee.

A concern for interpersonal effectiveness is probably even more crucial for personnel selection than for personnel development. The part time aspect of most continuing education instructional positions allows administrators to find out how well a teacher relates to adult students and to continue only those teachers who do well. This practice is widespread. The selection of a full time program administrator or a policy board member whose interpersonal relationships are unsatisfactory can create a long term problem.

Adults can become more effective in their interpersonal relations. Procedures to facilitate this process include supervisory coaching, feedback regarding especially effective or ineffective performances, sensitivity training and encounter groups, micro-teaching, and various forms of supervised clinical experience in which experience is combined with constructive feedback.

Approach to Practice

A third personal quality is the attitude of practitioners to improving their professional performance. This issue has been explored for professional development generally (Argyris and Schön, 1976; Schein, 1978) and for continuing education practitioners in particular (Ingham, 1972; Ingham and Hanks, 1978). Most people who have analyzed professional proficiency and performance conclude that effective practitioners must go beyond routine activities and reactions to external pressures. Without innovation and a sense of direction, practitioners tend to become obsolete and agencies tend to become stagnant (Gardner, 1964; Mezirow, 1978). As important as stability and routine may be as a platform for constructive change, an effective practitioner is typically creative and energetic in dealing with multiple target and program areas, vague priorities, uncertain policy mandates and bases for resource allocation, and competition from other providers. Under these circumstances, for example, an administrator is well served by qualities such as creativity and planning skills (Adelson, 1976; Cohen and March, 1974).

Much of the early analysis of creative imagination and problem solving stressed the importance of forestalling premature judgment which tends to foreclose some of the most imaginative and effective solutions or courses of action (Osborn, 1953). Openness to new and useful ways of thinking and acting are marks of imaginative practice. Creativity involves efforts to produce novel, beneficial, and especially appropriate results which transform our past perceptions and are rich in implications for future action.

Those who urge practitioners to improve their practice tend to emphasize the use of scientific methods and systems concepts to critique and evaluate program activities, and to develop and implement deliberate plans for improvement. The emphasis is usually on use of systematic procedures to guide reflective thought, generate plans, and solve problems (Davis, 1973; Miller, Galanter, and Pribram, 1960; Newell and Simon, 1972). However, as Simon (1969) has noted, the scientific concern for general explanations is insufficient for practitioners who seek action results in specific situations. Ingham (1972) concluded that practitioners should analyze both extant and changing circumstances (along with the impact of the practitioner on the change). Commentaries by Ruesch (1975) and Jantsch (1975) emphasize the valuable contributions to program improvement that lie beyond the scientific method. They refer to the importance of understanding connotations along with intuitive and holistic appreciations of events.

The ways in which most practitioners perform their roles tend to be quite intuitive and to include few deliberate efforts to improve practice systematically. Those who are more deliberate in their efforts tend to be above average in performance but also less satisfied with it than the typical practitioner. This leads to a commitment to strive and change. Program evaluation aimed at improvement can contribute to such commitment. This is especially so when qualitative information about expectations of various audiences are included in the evaluation process. Practitioners who have an effective approach to the constant improvement of practice are likely to be at the growing edge of the field.

use of proficiency

The various ways in which practitioners exhibit proficiencies in having a broad perspective on the field, in understanding adults as learners, and in personal qualities tend to be reflected in judgments regarding the extent of their professionalism. Such judgments are increasingly being made by policy makers and by committees of professional associations in the field. The following examples regarding goal setting, staffing, and collaboration indicate how such proficiencies can be useful.

Directors of public school adult education who seek to provide leadership in major goals and emphases for their program confront challenges both in the school system and in the community. With declining enrollments and financial support, school boards and administrators may either become hostile toward continuing education (as competition for scarce resources needed for the children), or more supportive of it (as essential for building and maintaining community support for the total school system). Much depends on how effective the director and other staff members are in setting goals and on the sense of direction they provide for continuing education.

The director's concern about goal setting may rise further if other agencies in the school district also have vigorous continuing education programs. If, for example, a community college district is established and receives state funds for continuing education programs which then may migrate from the school system to the community college, the director is likely to be quite concerned about his or her program and its role in the community.

Many of the capabilities reviewed in this chapter could contribute to the director's effectiveness in this situation. A perspective on the field can alert the director to the complementarity of agencies, to influences of funding patterns, and to ways in which directors elsewhere and in the past have used distinctive purposes and resources in their parent organization to successfully differentiate their programs from those of other providers. Access to statements that have been prepared about the goals and accomplishments of continuing education programs can provide the director with concepts and phrases that can contribute to persuasiveness. An understanding of agency functioning can help the director plan strategy to win support (Farmer and Knox, 1977; Mezirow, Darkenwald, and Knox, 1975). An awareness of staff development issues and procedures can enable the director to broaden the base of staff contribution to the goal setting process (Spear, 1976). An understanding of adults as learners can help the director emphasize the impact continuing education can make on the lives of local residents. Directors should also realize that their own enthusiasm for lifelong learning and their interpersonal effectiveness can make a major difference; should they lack these attributes, other staff members should be able to offer them.

Another example is provided by the director of an employer's education and training department who is concerned with the selection and development of trainers. Because supervisors are so influential in the achievement of goals for staff and organization development, the director must be concerned with their participation. If he or she was recently appointed—without much experience and background in training and continuing education—the experience and conclusions of training directors elsewhere would be greatly beneficial (Craig, 1976). A rationale taking into account both individual and organizational needs (Schein, 1978), and concepts and evidence regarding job enrichment might also be helpful (Hackman and others, 1975).

An understanding of the broad field of continuing education and of adults as learners could suggest some of the qualities to look for in selecting people to help plan and conduct training activities, and to emphasize in orientation activities. Information about other providers might help differentiate corporate requirements for personnel development to be met by other agencies from those to be met internally by programs conducted by the department. Information about career development and organizational behavior might help the director identify points at which educational programs are likely to make a difference.

A third example concerns the stance of a director of university continuing education regarding collaboration with other types of agencies. An understanding of the variety of learning projects and educational activities in which adults engage, along with variations among agencies in the characteristics of the adults they attract, might help the director recognize distinctive contributions of various agencies. Generalizations about community organization, organizational behavior, and patterns of adult information seeking might assist the director in collaboration and decisions regarding a backstopping role for his or her agency in some instances, in contrast with cosponsorship or independent programs. A commitment to the broad field can also help the director work through some of the interagency conflicts that are likely to occur. Reading a history of local continuing education councils and roundtables might also provide a perspective on their importance and difficulties.

In similar ways, teachers, counselors, and policy makers can use the types of capacities reviewed in this chapter to become more effective in the specific tasks that they confront.

summary

All categories of practitioners engaged in continuing education would benefit from three broad areas of proficiency: a comprehensive perspective on the field, an understanding of adults as learners, and personal qualities such as effective interpersonal relations. A comprehensive perspective on the field includes attention to types of providers, relationships between the agency and parent organization, societal influences such as trends and issues, and resource identification including literature, money, and people.

An understanding of adults as learners includes attention to both development and learning. Generalizations about adult development are especially useful to practitioners in relation to role performance, change events, information seeking, and self-concept. Generalizations about adult learning are especially useful to practitioners in relation to ability, meaning, adjustment, pacing, interference, reinforcement, and feedback.

Important personal qualities of effective practitioners include commitment, interpersonal effectiveness, and the desire to improve performance. Professional values include a commitment to the broad field of continuing education. Interpersonal effectiveness includes winning cooperation on which so much of practitioner effectiveness depends. An innovative approach to practice includes attention to creativity and problem solving.

These abilities are useful to practitioners in many ways, including goal setting, staffing, and collaboration. An understanding of these three areas of proficiency can help practitioners focus their efforts to become more effective. Additional proficiencies that are more specialized for administrators, resource persons, and policy makers are described in the next three chapters.

Major areas of proficiency of particular importance to administrators include administration, program development, and research.

administrators

Most of those who devote full time to continuing education of adults are in administrative roles. In addition to personal qualities and an understanding of the field and of adults as learners—important for all categories of practitioners—effective administrators tend to have some areas of proficiency specific for their roles. These include administration, program development, and the uses of research. They are a factor in the typical backgrounds of continuing education administrators, and impinge on their relationships with essentially part time instructional personnel.

The several categories of continuing education administrators in most agency settings each have their own demands. The agency director has the overall administrative responsibility for the continuing education function within the parent organization. Examples include the director of the education and training department for an employer, the director of adult education for a school system, the director of extension for a university, the director of adult religious education for a large religious institution, or the director of continuing education and community services for a community college. In a small agency, the director may be the only full time administrator. The major aspects of the position include relations with policy makers in the parent organization, with representatives of external groups, and with program administrators in the agency.

Another category of administrator is the program administrator. In smaller agencies, program administrators assist the director by working with program areas, usually organized around subject matter fields (business, agriculture, humanities), clientele groups (undereducated, women, senior citizens), or delivery systems (evening credit courses, guided individual study, conferences and institutes). In larger agencies, a program administrator may direct a section of the agency that includes other program administrators. An example is the director of conferences and institutes in which a number of conference coordinators are employed. Program administrators typically report to a continuing education administrator and work mainly with resource persons and representatives of client groups in the program development process.

Additional categories of administrative and support personnel are associated with many continuing education agencies. Some are employed by the agency, such as a business manager, registrar, or payroll clerk. Some are employed by the parent organization but devote a substantial portion of their effort to the continuing education function. Examples occur in support services such as personnel, library, admissions, instructional materials, and public information. It is often a matter of historical accident whether a business manager or a public information specialist concerned with marketing is located in the continuing education agency or elsewhere in the parent organization. Some affiliated personnel who perform administrative roles are located in other agencies. Included are people in cosponsoring or referral organizations (such as employment or welfare) who help with recruitment and referrals. Sometimes they have formal appointments and a part time salary. These other categories of administrative and support personnel typically make specialized contributions to the agency other than program development.

need for proficiency

Past efforts to specify current and needed proficiencies of continuing education administrators have reflected both expectations regarding excellent performance, and descriptions of the proficiencies that administrators typically have when they enter the field (Craven, 1964; Deppe, 1969; Farmer, 1970; Gossage, 1967; Griffith, 1970; Griffith and Hayes, 1970; Heroux, 1975; Jensen, 1969; Jensen, Liveright, and Hallenbeck, 1964; Kreitlow, 1965; Lauffer, 1977; Lippitt and Nadler, 1967; Madry, 1963; Marshall, 1968). Comments regarding expectations for excellent performance have been included earlier in this volume. They include understanding and commitment to adult learning and to the field and agency, along with interpersonal effectiveness. Given the great expectations for continuing education in contrast with the lack of policy and financial support that its practitioners typically confront, the demands on conscientious administrators are quite severe. In addition to expectations typical of administrators, those in our field are urged to produce results both as to numbers and quality, and to relate effectively to the parent organization and to the community although their agency is marginal to the parent organization. In addition, because most of the people who help adults learn do so on a part time basis, most administrators do not have a faculty as a collective group of experts who assume the main continuing responsibility for the educational program. As a result, many continuing education program administrators are more directly involved in program development activities than is the case for most other administrators of educational programs.

Continuing education administrators enter their first administrative position in the field with exceedingly diverse backgrounds. Many have had some previous contact with continuing education programs, often teaching adults. However, only a small proportion enter the field in any capacity with preparatory education specifically dealing with continuing education of adults. One exception is the Cooperative Extension Service of the Land Grant Universities in which many staff members have some course work in extension education. In public school adult education, many directors have administrator's certificates and the related preparation in school administration that is required. However, most practitioners enter the field with little relevant formal education in continuing education, but often with both education and experience that is pertinent to at least some professional tasks.

There appears to be no other field of study and experience from which a major proportion of continuing education administrators come. Some of the fields that are moderately well represented are teaching, administration, social and behavioral sciences, and health professions. Many of those who become continuing education administrators gained some administrative or leadership experience in other settings, sometimes in voluntary associations. With this diversity of background, a concern for proficiencies of continuing education administrators includes attention to both the tasks they are to perform and the background they typically bring to the role. Therefore, the following section on areas of proficiency includes attention to both typical and desirable proficiencies.

areas of proficiency

In addition to the general capabilities of all categories of practitioners, there are three areas of proficiency with special importance for continuing education administrators. They are administration, program development, and the use of research. In each area, there is a gap between desirable and typical abilities and a need to augment the latter (Jensen, Liveright, and Hallenbeck, 1964; Shaw, 1969).

Administration

Continuing education administrators share basic functions with those in other fields: working with and through others to achieve agreement on important goals and encouraging them to make contributions to that end. These are the basic functions of leadership in any setting. Within the context of the continuing education agency, parent organization, and community, administrative leadership also entails dealing with organizational stability and change.

Continuing education administration is an art based on a science. The art of administration entails concern for responsiveness, interpersonal relations, and humanistic values that should guide professional practice. Effective practice is based on science because it draws upon research based generalizations from various scholarly disciplines, and orderly procedures that contribute to effectiveness. The art and the science of administration are complementary. Both depend on experience with people, relationships in the specific situation, and concepts from the organized knowledge of the field.

Administration includes at least four general components in addition to program development. They are attraction and retention of participants, acquisition and allocation of resources, staff selection and development, and leadership including planning and coordination.

Participation. Marketing and counseling practices to attract and retain adult learners are intended to focus and accelerate their information seeking. Participation rates increase with level of formal education (Boaz, 1978; Johnstone and Rivera, 1965; Okes, 1976). Especially for reaching the underserved, marketing efforts are more likely to be effective if they are specifically targeted (Anderson and Niemi, 1969). Participation in continuing education is encouraged by marketing and counseling services which seek to affect personal and situational influences (Knox and Farmer, 1977). An understanding of specific major influences on continuing education participation helps specify an adult's force field which administrators seek to affect (Miller, 1967). Personal characteristics (such as educational level) and situational characteristics (such as accessibility of information) have been identified as important influences (Parker and Paisley, 1966). Other major influences include encouragement by friends and acquaintances and cosponsorship by organizations to which potential participants belong (London, Wenkert, and Hagstrom, 1963). The reasons for adults to participate in continuing education vary with people and activities, and multiple reasons are typical. The most usual reason is the wish to achieve goals in work, family, or community. Other major reasons are interest in the content and enjoyment of the association with other participants (Boshier, 1977; Houle, 1961).

Concepts and procedures for marketing of services of non-profit organizations apply fairly well to continuing education (Kotler, 1974). Marketing entails a responsive client-orientation which emphasizes a mutually beneficial exchange between the agency and its publics. For continuing education this includes potential participants, potential resource persons, and policy makers. Proficient administrators are able to plan and conduct effective marketing activities. Included are marketing audit of relevant organizational missions and resources, analysis of educational needs of each major target market, a description of the current and forecasted situation, alternative marketing strategies, proposed action targets, and marketing budget. Ingredients of the marketing strategy include attention to the programs that are provided, along with price, place, and promotion. Promotion tools include advertising, publicity, personal contact, and incentives.

Effective administrators seek retention as well as attraction of participants. There are various contributors to participant persistence (Boshier, 1973; Houle, 1964). One is the usefulness of the continuing education program. In addition, counseling services can contribute to continued participation (Farmer, 1971; Perrone and Davis, 1976), such as provision of information about educational and career opportunities, assessment of interests and abilities, assistance to plan sequences of courses, discussion about personal problems and possible solutions, referral advocacy on behalf of clients. Although there are some professional counselors who assist current and potential participants, most of the counseling function is provided by program administrators and teachers as a small part of their roles. In some locales assistance is provided by community-based counseling or brokering centers (Heffernan, Macy, and Vickers, 1976).

Administrative proficiency in marketing and counseling services is important because most agencies are so very dependent upon a continuous flow of satisfied adult participants for their survival. When participation is voluntary and there are multiple providers, responsiveness to client needs is crucial to success. Administrators may use this capability directly to plan and conduct marketing and counseling activities, or may use it indirectly to select and supervise specialists who do so within the agency or on a contract basis from outside the agency.

In practice, most continuing education administrators are keenly interested in marketing and new enrollments but less interested in counseling and persistence of current participants. With just a little experience, administrators can discover that word of mouth mention of a program by satisfied participants is one of the most potent influences on new enrollments. It is generally assumed that this informal recruitment just happens and that there is little an administrator can do about it. However, some administrators have been able to locate people who can help with such oral communication. The most widespread deliberate marketing procedures entail use of mass media such as brochures and newspaper listings of offerings. Because the harder to reach members of many target markets of adults tend not to use mass media for instrumental information seeking and tend not to know continuing education participants, these marketing approaches contribute to the largely middle-class clientele for continuing education (Anderson and Niemi, 1969; London, Wenkert, and Hagstrom, 1963). Except in adult basic education, counseling services are little used to reach and retain underserved adults. Although administrators and other agency staff members perform some counseling functions, such as at registration time, little systematic attention has been given to the continuing education counseling function (Knox and Farmer, 1977).

Resources. In addition to recruitment of participants and acquisition of staff, continuing education agencies require various financial and physical resources along with volunteer and in-kind contributions. Resources include income (from participant fees, tax support, external grant funds) and subsidy by the parent organization or cosponsors in the form of free provision of facilities, equipment, materials, and volunteer services. Some resources such as facilities and materials may also be acquired by continuing education funds or may be rented.

A time consuming component of administration is acquisition and allocation of resources. Practitioner effectiveness in this process entails taking into account influences on the agency such as its image, established sources of funding, and competition from other providers. The image of an agency as worthy of support from potential participants and policy makers contributes to the ongoing acquisition of participants and staff as well as of resources for which the administrator must continually arrange. Financial policies and arrangements, including legislative appropriations, vary with the type of parent organization of which the agency is a part (Dorland, 1969; Kidd, 1962; Pitchell, 1974).

Resource acquisition procedures include preparation of a budget request within the parent organization, fees paid by participants, financial assistance and vouchers for participants, and preparation of proposals for external grants. A continuing concern of very effective administrators is the allocation of resources to achieve agency objectives. This is aided by including those who administer budgets in the budget making process. Accounting concepts and procedures can also help an administrator monitor and influence staff performance, expenditures, and inventories (Hentschke, 1975).

An understanding of and ability to use concepts and procedures for resource acquisition and allocation enables an administrator to maintain satisfactory agency stability and to facilitate the achievement of agency objectives. In practice, there is a tendency for tasks related to resource acquisition and allocation to take so much of the administrator's time and energy that little is left over for program development. As a result many continuing education agencies are not very innovative. Innovative administrators tend to use procedures such as program budgeting or grant acquisition in ways that relate program activities and resources closely to goals and impact. Although financial assistance to adult participants has been much discussed in the field, this continues to be a major problem in many segments of the field.

Staffing. One of the most important components of administration is the attraction, selection, and development of staff—including teachers, counselors, administrators, and support staff. Included in the process is enrichment of talent pools, preparation of position descriptions, creation of positions that are attractive regarding the work itself and related benefits, and selection procedures to screen and select applicants (Beach, 1975; Flippo, 1976). Staff and organization development includes activities aimed at individual performance (Grabowski, 1976; Harris and Bessent, 1969; Knox, 1971; Kozoll, 1974; Spear, 1976) and at agency effectiveness (Beckhard, 1969; Bennis, 1969; SREB, 1971). Participation in staff and organization development appears to increase with the professionalization and effectiveness of continuing education administrators (Mezirow, Darkenwald, and Knox, 1975).

An administrator who is proficient regarding staffing activities is able to attract, retain, and develop talented staff members, especially those who help adults learn. It is upon staff performance that agency success mainly depends (Sager, 1963). The most effective approaches to staffing have emphasized a systemic approach in which effective supervision (Sergiovanni, 1971) is combined with strategies for organizational change (Lindquist, 1978; Porter, 1970). For a director, this approach begins with the selection of program administrators and administrators within the parent organization (Goldstein and Sorcher, 1973), and helps them to become more effective as knowledge brokers and change agents (Havelock and Havelock, 1972). In doing so, attention can be given to both individual concern for satisfaction and career development, and organizational concern for productivity (Hackman and Oldham, 1975; Hall, 1976; Schein, 1978; Schneider, 1976; Van Maanen, 1977).

In practice, continuing education administrators tend to be committed in principle to the importance of staff development for instructional, administrative, and support personnel associated with their agency but to devote relatively little effort to it. Because so many agency staff members are part time, their lack of availability and commitment makes it difficult to schedule staff development activities. Because it is easier to phase out unsatisfactory personnel who work part time than those who work full time, selective retention instead of staff development tends to be a major way of maintaining quality of performance. In those instances in which continuing education administrators have conducted especially effective staff and organization development activities they have typically used procedures that are effective for continuing education program development generally. Some of the most effective efforts have produced high levels of enthusiasm, loyalty, and innovativeness by encouraging program administrators and instructors to become more creative in their efforts and not solely follow organizational expectations. In general, the areas of proficiency described in Chapter Four can serve as the basis for selection and development of instructional personnel.

Leadership. In addition to proficient performance of the foregoing administrative functions, leadership entails coordination so that in concert the individual programs are well conducted and the total agency achieves its objectives and runs smoothly (Katz and Kahn, 1966). Effective leadership reflects an understanding of organizational behavior, program productivity, priority setting, and administrative strategies (Caplow, 1967; Cohen and March, 1974; Drucker, 1966). The core of administration is decision making which takes into account both organizational productivity and individual satisfaction (Blake and Mouton, 1964). Decision making is only partly a formal, rational process. It also reflects legal requirements along with political and bureaucratic influences (Allison, 1971). Organizational theory and role theory can help an administrator understand the interweaving of stability and change in expectations and performance, including identification of likely strategic influences (Biddle and Thomas, 1966; Burns and Stalker, 1961; Lindquist, 1978). Administration entails working with individuals and groups with differing views of goals and procedures. Effective coordination includes attention to these differences regarding priorities, resource allocation, program balance, dealing with opposition, and tradeoffs. Procedures for provision of both monetary and nonmonetary incentives, especially for resource persons, are among the most subtle and important in administration. Recent efforts to approach personnel development through organization development are especially promising (Lindquist, 1978; Schein, 1978).

In practice, continuing education administrators tend to devote much of their effort to the maintenance of stability through making ad hoc arrangements for facilities, participants, resource persons, materials, money, and cooperative working relationships (Hoppe, 1969). Just as in rolling a boulder up a mountain, failure to persist has negative consequences. The power poor position of most continuing education administrators within their parent organization makes it difficult to increase organizational commitment and achieve organizational change. Administrative influence reflects many qualities including time investment (Mintzberg, 1973), a sense of direction (Apps, 1973), and persistence in the face of inertia and resistance (Cohen and March, 1974). Continuing education administrators tend to be unfamiliar with the traditions and literature of the field. However, what they may lack in concern for the past and future tends to be at least partly made up for in their intense concern for current results. A type of missionary spirit attracts many practitioners to the field and contributes to a commitment to responsive programming. When this is combined with effective program development procedures, it may produce continuing education programs which are educationally sound and have impact.

Program priorities are actually set by various categories of people associated with an agency. Emphases emerge as policy boards endorse or support some recommendations but not others, clients enroll in some courses or workshops but not others, resource persons select topics and instructional procedures, outside organizations agree to become cosponsors, and administrators engage in consensus building, staffing, and resource allocation. In general, administrators can encourage policy makers to acquire competencies described in Chapter Five of this sourcebook.

Over the years, policy boards for the parent organization have given relatively little attention to the continuing education function, but in recent years this has been changing. Report requirements related to external funding can also influence program priorities. Effective administrators realize the importance of these many ways of setting priorities and strive to do so continuously and unobtrusively (Houle, 1960; Richman and Farmer, 1974). Administrative coordination to achieve program objectives depends heavily on effective communication (Knox, 1975). Within the agency, effective administrators focus on team building in which objectives, resource allocation, and working relationships all influence results. Outside the parent organization and service area, communication entails both use of existing informal information channels and of public information aimed at both potential participants and supporters (Beckerman, 1972). This can also include attention to the variety of continuing education agencies in the service area, and the contribution of associations and councils to facilitate interagency relations (Beder, 1978). Over the years, successful continuing education administrators have related well with client groups. In recent years it has become more important to relate well with people in the parent organization and in other agencies (Knox, 1975).

Under these circumstances, an important aspect of leadership is innovation. Practitioners have available a growing literature on this topic that can enrich their strategies (Baldridge and Deal, 1975; Darkenwald, 1977; Farmer and Knox, 1977; House, 1974).

Program Development

To some extent program development is the concern of everyone associated with a continuing education agency. However, for program administrators, planning and conducting learning activities for adults is the core of their effort (Havelock, 1969). The specifics vary for the university extension conference coordinator, the employer's education and training department trainer for supervisory training, the community college coordinator of continuing education programs for women, and the professional association staff member who arranges workshops and meetings for the membership. However, all must deal with five basic components of program development as they work with planning committees, relate to potential participants and to resource persons, prepare materials, and orient those who conduct continuing education programs. Two significant components in the origination of ideas for new programs are needs assessment and analysis of contextual resources and influences. Other components are selection of high priority objectives, selection and organization of learning activities, and program evaluation.

The proficiency of a program administrator in program development activities entails more than having evolved concepts and procedures that fit the expectations and routines of an agency (Leagans, Copeland, and Kaiser, 1971). One of the additional considerations is the interpersonal setting in which the program occurs. In the individual setting, such as a correspondence course or on-the-job coaching, the individual learner has a minimum of interaction with other learners. In the temporary group setting, such as an evening course, the participants typically have had little previous contact. In the organizational setting, such as organization development for employees, the program reflects their previous interaction and efforts to alter organizational functioning. In the community setting, such as community development, program ideas evolve from problems and opportunities related to two or more organizations or segments of a neighborhood or community where a major program purpose is community improvement. One indication of a high level of program development proficiency is the ability to adapt procedures to fit each setting or combination of settings (Pennington and Green, 1976; Tyler, 1950; Whipple, 1957). Examples include adaptation of workshop procedures typical for middle-class participants when working with undereducated adults, or adaptation of rural community development procedures when working in urban areas.

Needs. Information about educational needs is a major source of ideas for the creation or modification of programs. Most practitioners draw ideas for new programs from local personal experience (Pennington and Green, 1976). Proficient practitioners use somewhat more formal procedures for needs assessment, which entail use of several methods of obtaining information about educational needs (Bradshaw, 1974; McKinley, 1973; Monette, 1977). The types of information include: expressed preferences by potential participants, demonstrated willingness to respond to programs when offered, conclusions of experts regarding educational needs of a category of adults, evidence from those who are affected by the proficiency level of a category of adults (such as patients regarding needs of nurses), and proficiency level as compared with similar adults. Among the sources of information about educational needs of adults are historical, philosophical, and operational traditions (Apps, 1973; Knowles, 1977; Smith, Aker, and Kidd, 1970), societal and agency context (Mezirow, Darkenwald, and Knox, 1975), emerging social, political, and economic trends (Freire, 1970), an exploration of likely and desirable alternative futures (Ziegler, 1970), and an understanding of adult development (Havighurst and Orr, 1956; Knox, 1977a).

Effective use of needs assessment procedures is important for several reasons. Such procedures operationalize practitioner commitment to being learner centered, provide a major basis for effective marketing activities, and help keep the growing edge of an agency alive. A proficient administrator uses needs assessment procedures effectively and helps resource persons to acquire concepts and procedures that enable them to do so as well. Needs assessment procedures can be used to identify new program areas which an agency initiates, and new target markets to serve, as well as to plan specific courses or workshops.

In practice, most continuing education administrators use quite rudimentary needs assessment procedures such as asking a question on course reaction forms to obtain suggestions for new programs, noting enrollment trends for new offerings in similar agency and community settings, and use of survey forms. Two effective procedures that are underutilized are combining several procedures to cross validate conclusions about high priority educational needs, and carefully evaluating pilot projects designed to explore latent needs.

Context. Most continuing education programs are planned and conducted within the context of the providing agency, along with the organizational or community context in which the participants function. This context includes influences on the clientele that encourage or discourage them from participating in continuing education activities and from applying what they learn. The context also contains resources that can be used to plan and conduct programs. Included are the purposes and resources of the providing agency. Proficient program administrators are able to inventory these resources and influences, and to reflect them in the continuing education activities.

Effective analysis of contextual resources and influences is important for several reasons. A program is more likely to be successful if it fits the educational needs of the clientele and the purposes and resources of the providing agency. The offerings of other providers in the service area can also be influential. A proficient administrator is able to take such resources and influences readily into account along with the major sources of encouragement and discouragement which affect participation and application by the clientele.

In practice, many program administrators concentrate mainly on estimates of client needs when deciding on new programs and give little attention to purposes and resources of the parent organization, and even less to other providers. In areas where practitioners have formed councils and round-tables, there tends to be somewhat greater concern for complementarity and collaboration. Practitioner concern for facilitators and barriers that affect participation and application tends to occur mainly in programs developed in organization and community settings, in contrast with individual and temporary group settings. Concern for influences on participation tends also to be high in special projects designed to reach underserved adults. Agencies that emphasize marketing are also likely to analyze situational influences on participation.

Objectives. The origins of a program idea typically yield more potential objectives than can be feasibly accommodated in a single continuing education course or workshop. Objective setting consists of screening potential objectives for desirability and feasibility, and establishing a clear and realistic set of educational objectives to which both potential participants and resource persons are committed. In best practice the objective setting process includes a program administrator, resource persons with content competence, and some representative potential participants. Although objectives are sometimes stated in terms of instructor purposes or institutional goals, it is more useful for program planning and marketing to state objectives in terms of intended participant knowledge, skills, and attitudes along with subject matter content (Mager, 1962). For some programs, the set of objectives taken together indicate desirable shifts in actual performance. Effective procedures for objectives setting typically provide opportunities for participants to help modify the objectives as required by the activity (Knowles, 1970).

A program administrator who is proficient in objective setting is able to make a number of valuable contributions to program development. One of them is to include, on a planning committee or similar arrangement, the people whose contributions are necessary to produce a set of important and acceptable objectives. Another is to help state clear and realistic objectives that the learners should achieve. Such wording contributes to program planning and marketing. A third is to help those who conduct continuing education programs to effectively use procedures (such as agenda building) which enable them to build consensus among participants and resource persons regarding program objectives, and to modify objectives if necessary as the program progresses (Knowles, 1970; Knox, 1974).

In practice, continuing education courses and workshops tend to be more focused regarding clientele benefits and program purposes than is the case for much of preparatory education. Many program brochures and related materials give a fairly good idea of what the program is designed to accomplish, even though a clear list of intended learner outcomes is not included. In some segments of the field, such as continuing education for nurses, there has been a strong emphasis on stating behavioral objectives. Too little attention is typically given at the outset of most programs to clarification and consensus building regarding objectives by participants as well as resource persons. Many continuing education programs are so tightly scheduled that it is difficult to modify objectives and activities even if it proves desirable.

Activities. There are dozens and dozens of learning activities that have been used in continuing education programs, each with different instructional methods and materials (Klevins, 1972; Miller, 1964). Proficient program administrators select from this range those that are most appropriate for the objectives and participants, and organize the activities so that they are effective regarding stage and pacing of the total program (Houle, 1972). Five criteria for selection of learning activities are: appropriateness for the objectives and content, suitability for the clientele, effectiveness in relation to the stage of a program, pacing and variety, and compatibility with teaching style (Joyce and Weil, 1972; Knox, 1974; Solomon, Bezdek, and Rosenberg, 1963; Travers, 1973). Additional concepts of importance to proficient program planners are individualization of instruction, use of participatory learning activities such as case discussion (Stenzel and Feeney, 1970), and encouragement of application of new learnings through changed performance.

For the program administrator, proficiency in selection and organization of learning activities is especially important at three points in the program development process: when deciding on the general program plan, when selecting and orienting resource persons, and when conducting program evaluation to improve the program.

In practice, continuing education program administrators typically share decisions regarding learning activities with resource persons. Even though they usually have a more active role than in preparatory education, many are less influential than they might be in helping to design learning activities. Most of the resource persons who help adults learn do so on a part time basis, and many of them are unfamiliar with the wide range of learning activities from which they could select (Biddle and Biddle, 1965; Bradford, Gibb, and Benne, 1964; Cross and Valley, 1974; Johnson, 1965; Lawrence and Lorsch, 1969; Mathieson, 1971). Program administrators are more likely to be familiar with learner concerns and interactive methods for teaching and learning, and to be able to share this information with resource persons and others engaged in the planning process.

Evaluation. Proficient practitioners use formal program evaluation procedures to supplement the informal evaluation that always occurs (Stake, 1967; Worthen and Sanders, 1973). Program evaluation is a process of making judgments, based on evidence, regarding program worth and effectiveness, in ways that encourage persons associated with the program to use the conclusions for program improvement and justification (Knox, 1969). Evaluation activities include planning, selecting, describing, judging, and reporting (Grotelueschen, Gooler, and Knox, 1976). A feasible evaluation project is typically smaller than the wide range of evaluation purposes and components that might be included, so focusing is required. The emphasis might be on internal formative evaluation which encourages persons associated with the program to use findings for program improvement largely within their control. By contrast, external summative evaluation emphasizes impartial judgments about outcomes, the achievement of objectives, and unintended consequences, for purposes of justification and accountability (Kent, 1973). Many of the most effective program evaluations combine both internal and external evaluation (Steele, 1973).

Continuing education administrators who are proficient in evaluation provide active leadership for program evaluation and improvement (Knox and others, 1974). Such leadership pertains to commitment of staff time and related resources, facilitation of data collection and analysis, encouragement of use of findings, and judgments about the adequacy of the evaluation and evaluators (Stufflebeam, 1974). Proficiency in program evaluation is important because the resultant responsiveness and improvement is so necessary to the success of the agency.

In practice, continuing education administrators tend to be dismayed by misuses of evaluation (exams and grades) in preparatory education, to be overwhelmed by the seeming complexity of proposed evaluation procedures, and to feel guilty about not doing a more effective job of program evaluation. Heavy reliance is placed on enrollment trends, drop out rates, financial summaries, and participant opinionnaires as data for making judgments about program effectiveness and worth. In some segments of the field, such as the Cooperative Extension Service and industrial training, attention has been given to practice adoption as evidence of program impact. Especially when associated with externally funded projects, some practitioners have conducted some very useful program evaluation projects.

Uses of Research

Two decades ago, a review of research in education of adults revealed few important studies that dealt specifically with aspects of continuing education but quite a few from other fields which contributed useful generalizations (Brunner and others, 1959). Today, the amount of useful research based generalizations related to education of adults has increased enormously (Niemi, Grabowski, and Kuusisto, 1976). Very little of this research has been produced by practitioners in the field, who tend to be very action oriented. However, continuing education administrators are in a central position in the production and utilization of findings from research and evaluation. Thus it is important to consider the typical and desirable proficiencies related to research possessed by continuing education administrators.

Much of the research on continuing education can be subsumed within four broad topic areas: adults as learners, program development, agency organization and administration, and societal trends and issues related to lifelong learning (Knox, 1977b). Some of this research has been conducted by people who identify closely with the field of continuing education. A few of them were practitioners when they conducted the research, but most were professors and graduate students in the approximately eighty graduate programs in North America with specializations in adult and continuing education. However, the majority of relevant research has been conducted by researchers from various fields whose scholarly interests at some points intersected with some aspect of continuing education. The resulting relationship between researcher and practitioner in continuing education is therefore more tenuous than in other fields, such as between economics and business administration, or political science and public administration. As a result, an important area of proficiency for continuing education administrators is the ability to convey, to various types of researchers, practitioner concerns as an input to research planning. Equally important is an adequate understanding of research completed so as to facilitate its use and application. If full time administrators do not know about and adapt relevant research findings to local planning and decision making, few other people associated with the agency are likely to do so.

There are several ways in which a familiarity with continuing education research procedures and findings would be useful to administrators. Some research and evaluation procedures can be used for agency evaluation and for purposes beyond the evaluation of the teaching-learning transaction component in program development. Awareness of findings from research and evaluation studies provides a broader perspective from which to interpret local evaluation findings. Research and evaluation findings related to results help to justify program efforts, and research and evaluation related to process help to improve procedures. Some research findings help to identify crucial aspects of a problem, and some help to identify alternative solutions. A familiarity with sources of research reports and summaries can enable an administrator to efficiently locate relevant generalizations regarding both topic and degree of detail. A familiarity with research procedures can enable an administrator to draw useful conclusions from research reports with a minimum of overgeneralizations (Fox, 1969; Kerlinger, 1973). The foregoing proficiencies related to research and evaluation can also enable an administrator to participate in research projects and to provide leadership to relate research and practice more closely.

In practice, very few administrators who have not themselves conducted research projects are much involved either as producers or consumers of research. This reflects more than lack of understanding and commitment on the part of practitioners. It partly reflects the scattered nature of research reports and summaries related to continuing education, and the lack of clear connections between organized knowledge from research and the action problems and opportunities that mainly concern practitioners. When research findings have been summarized and presented in a form that is useful to continuing education practitioners, they have been fairly responsive.

increasing proficiency

There are various ways in which continuing education administrators can and do increase their professional proficiency. Professional growth is an especially important consideration because, unlike practitioners in most professions, very few enter the field with a common background of education or experience which might provide perspectives, major concepts, or standards of practice. By contrast, they often do bring distinctive viewpoints from their exceedingly different education and work experiences, a commitment to helping adults learn, and, ironically, an enthusiasm for discovering for themselves concepts and procedures already widely known in the field. The four main ways in which continuing education administrators increase their professional proficiency are: interaction with agency tasks and personnel, participation in continuing education associations, self-directed study, and graduate study. Each means of increasing proficiency can make a distinctive contribution. The outstanding practitioners in the field use most of them, in combination with a creative and caring and energetic approach to life.

Agency

The agency itself is the first and most important teacher for many continuing education administrators who drifted into the continuing education agency from another part of the parent organization. For example, the initial contact is, typically, teaching or administration in educational institutions, administration or personnel work in companies, and nursing in hospitals. To be sure, some administrators join a continuing education agency without prior experience and allegiance to the parent organization, but they appear to be in the minority.

As with most interesting jobs, the early years as a continuing education administrator hold much potential for professional growth. The tasks are varied and complex, and contain problems to be solved and opportunities to be pursued. Other agency personnel typically provide informal orientation regarding standard procedures and can engage in informal discussion about new program ideas. Some agencies have more formal arrangements to help staff members to become more proficient, but it is ironic that agencies that help others engage in personnel and organization development provide so little for their own staff. In addition to staff meetings and retreats, agencies could make greater use of task forces on special projects, program evaluation, shifts in assignments, marketing audits, outside consultants, and explorations of alternative futures as ways to increase administrative competence and enhance agency vitality.

Association

After a few years, a continuing education administrator is likely to join a professional association which leads to contact with colleagues in other agencies. Almost every segment of the field has at least one such specialized association, and there are some, such as the Adult Education Association, that include members from all segments of the field. The contact may be tangential, such as reading an association-produced newsletter or journal or attending an association-sponsored meeting or workshop. For a few, the contact is central and includes active participation and leadership in a range of association activities. Especially for the more active members, participation in a continuing education association contributes in several ways to increased professional proficiency. Included are exposure to new ideas and practices, encouragement regarding standards of effective practice, and visibility for mobility in the field.

Self-Directed Study

Along with other American adults, almost all continuing education administrators engage in self-directed learning projects each year. For the general adult population, the average is five distinct learning projects each year totaling hundreds of hours (Tough, 1978). Given the educational level and type of occupation of continuing education administrators, their average amount of self-directed study is much above the average for the general population, and the proportion that is occupationally related is likely to be higher yet. Thus one of the main ways that many administrators increase their proficiency is through self-directed study. One means is reading; the professional literature has increased dramatically in recent decades. However, much more could be done to assist self-directed study through reading lists, study guides, video and audio tapes, consultation services, and self-assessment inventories (Knox, 1974).

Graduate Study

Thousands of administrators have completed a master's or doctoral degree program with a major in adult and continuing education, and many times that number have taken a few graduate courses. The upswing of graduates has been dramatic during the past two decades; about eighty university graduate programs now produce hundreds of graduates each year. Professors and graduate students in these programs also produce publications and conduct thousands of meetings and workshops that reach many practitioners in the field. Unlike agency activities and self-directed study, but like some association participation, graduate programs tend to emphasize exposure to concepts and procedures from throughout the field of continuing education and from related fields and scholarly disciplines that can broaden the perspective and enrich the performance of practitioners. Some of the graduate programs include internships and special seminars designed to help students develop their repertoire of strategies for alternating between action problems and knowledge resources. Some of the outstanding practitioners in the field have used their in-depth study to good advantage.

future directions

Increased proficiency by continuing education administrators can occur in various ways. Practitioners themselves can take direct action as individuals, as members of agencies, and as members of professional associations. Policy decisions can be made, such as agency support for administrators to become more proficient or university support for graduate programs with a specialization in continuing education. Research can be conducted to produce findings useful for action and policy making. This concluding section of the chapter presents desirable future directions for such efforts to increase proficiencies of continuing education administrators.

Direct Action

One action would be for more continuing education administrators to understand and use available marketing procedures so as to reach adults more effectively. Administrative commitment to this goal is widespread in the field. Information about pertinent marketing procedures is available (Kotler, 1974). Circumstances seem propitious for rapid progress.

A second desirable action would be for practitioners to engage in concerted effort to increase the sources of and information about financial assistance to adult participants. Although some policy changes are needed, such as broadened entitlements or access by part time students to scholarship and loan funds, there are some very effective financial assistance efforts scattered throughout the field that could readily be emulated by administrators elsewhere. Examples include participants and former participants who establish financial assistance funds in an agency, and employers and labor unions that encourage workers to use negotiated educational benefits, which are greatly underutilized (Levine, 1977).

A third action would be for practitioners to use effective procedures in staff and organization development for administrators in their own agencies. The examples are likely to be even more persuasive than the precepts.

A fourth desirable action would be for administrators to give more deliberate attention to relationships with policy makers. Awareness of major areas of proficiency by both administrators and policy makers can contribute to more mutually satisfactory relationships, which can further enhance the proficiencies of both. Fortunately, although continuing education practitioners are relatively powerless, they do have potentially greater access to policy makers than do administrators in most fields. This occurs in personal contact, in preparation of written reports, and especially by inclusion of policy makers as participants and resource persons in continuing education programs.

Use of formal needs assessment procedures, and other ways to originate new programs is a fifth action related to proficiencies of administrators. There is evidence that use of combinations of needs assessment procedures is associated with program success (Farmer and Knox, 1977). Continuing education directors can encourage and assist program administrators to become more proficient in the use of effective needs assessment procedures.

A sixth type of task for which improvement seems desirable is the use by program administrators of procedures for achieving greater consensus among resource persons and participants regarding high priority objectives. This action, along with the seventh and eighth that follow, call especially for leadership by continuing education directors. The seventh action would be to provide the support and facilitation needed for program evaluation worth the investment in terms of agency improvement and justification. The eighth action would be to relate research and practice more closely. Agency directors are in a strategic position to identify needed research and to use findings. Practitioners who have some proficiency regarding research and evaluation are more likely to collaborate with researchers on projects which will contribute to practice. The experience can also contribute much to increased proficiency.

Policy Issues

There are three policy issues that relate especially to proficiencies of continuing education administrators. To begin with, how much effort are agencies and society willing to invest in marketing to reach and teach underserved adults? Current policies and practices emphasize reaching the most participants with the least resources. The victims of this policy are those harder to reach who require far more effort to attract and retain. If priorities for serving harder to reach adults are sufficiently high, increased proficiency in regard to appropriate marketing procedures and to changes in the basis for resource allocation will be required.

A second policy issue, alluded to earlier, has to do with the current policies for financial assistance which discriminate against the part time student. Practitioners who can successfully change existing policies so that they provide greater benefits to continuing education participants are likely to command persuasive rationales and procedures for institutional change.

The third policy issue has to do with compartmentalization of the field. Practitioners in each segment have distinctive concepts and practices of great value to practitioners in others. Some graduate programs, professional associations, and publications have contributed to such sharing across segments of the field. One of the fundamental issues confronting administrators is their commitment and expertise in furthering coherence and vitality in their field rather than its fragmentation.

Research Questions

Four research questions illustrate the many which could contribute to policy making and action by continuing education administrators (Knox, 1977b). (1) Which marketing procedures tend to be most effective to attract and retain harder to reach adults, given various program objectives and target markets? (2) What combinations of needs assessment procedures tend to be most effective to efficiently identify high priority educational needs of adults, and how are the procedures related to characteristics of target markets and subsequent components of the program development process? (3) What is the impact of continuing education participation on adult role performance, and what feasible evaluation indicators can be used in practice to validly estimate that impact? (4) What are effective program development strategies by program administrators in relation to resource persons and clients? Current assumptions and generalizations about proficiencies of continuing education administrators help to suggest these research questions. Findings from such studies are likely to contribute to increased proficiency as well as to a better sense of the relative importance of proficiencies. In addition, the process of trying to ask and answer such questions can contribute to the innovativeness of continuing education administrators, which is a desirable area of proficiency.

summary

Continuing education administrators include agency directors, program administrators, and persons who perform other specialized administrative roles. Three important areas of proficiency are administration, program development, and the use of research. The art and science of administration includes attention to participation, resources, staffing, and leadership. Marketing and counseling activities help to attract and retain adult participants. Administrators devote much of their effort to acquisition and allocation of resources, including budgeting, proposal preparation, and obtaining funds from various sources. Decisions regarding staff selection and development are crucial to agency success. Administrative leadership entails planning and coordination to facilitate staff satisfaction and productivity.

Effective continuing education administrators give special attention to program development, which entails five components: needs, context, objectives, activities, and evaluation. Highly proficient administrators tend to use more formal needs assessment procedures which entail cross validation. Proficient administrators utilize relevant resources and influences in the context of program development to encourage adults to learn and apply what they learn. They also seek to achieve consensus on high priority objectives, to select from a range of learning abilities those that emphasize active learner participation, and to provide leadership regarding program evaluation. Although continuing education administrators are action oriented, they can make important contributions to the production and consumption of research.

The next two chapters provide parallel considerations of major areas of proficiency for resource persons and for policy makers.

Teachers and counselors who help adults learn need to be knowledgeable about subject matter content and adult development, as well as be capable in the use of program development procedures.

teachers and counselors

Some people associated with continuing education are mainly engaged in helping adults learn. Most of them do so on a part time basis as teachers and counselors. They are similar in their direct contact with adult learners and in their mentor role. The mentor role deals with the decisions related to five program development components described earlier: needs, context, objectives, activities, and evaluation. Most of them serve as experts and resource persons in planning and conducting educational activities such as courses, workshops, and guided individual study.

For continuing education agencies that are part of educational institutions such as schools, community colleges, and universities, a major source of resource persons consists of full time teachers in the preparatory education programs of the parent organization who also teach part time through the continuing education agency. Typically, less than half of the preparatory education faculty members teach in continuing education activities. In some educational institutions with enrollment declines in recent years there has been a small increase in the proportion of faculty members who teach continuing education courses for part time students as part of their regular academic load. In community colleges with a unified day and evening credit course program, many faculty members teach evening courses composed mainly of adult part time students. In the Cooperative Extension Service, county extension advisers conduct many educational programs but also utilize extension specialists from the faculty of the land grant university and many local volunteers.

However, the majority of those who conduct continuing education activities in educational institutions, especially non-credit activities such as workshops, are not full time faculty members (Williams, 1972). They are drawn from many sources. Some are faculty members from other institutions. In occupationally related continuing education programs, a majority are outstanding practitioners. In programs in the arts, many are practicing painters, musicians, and dancers. Governmental officials, homemakers, and people in all types of occupations are included as resource persons in continuing education. Some programs, especially those that receive external funding and meet during the daytime such as some adult basic education and vocational education programs, have hired full time teachers of adults in recent years.

The counseling function of continuing education agencies tends to be diffuse. It is performed by various categories of personnel (Knox and Farmer, 1977). A few agencies hire professionally prepared counselors, especially the urban university evening colleges and large adult basic education programs with a learning laboratory and daytime classes (Vontress and Thomas, 1968). Some agencies, such as those in community colleges and at places of employment, use counseling personnel from the parent organization. Much of the counseling function is performed not by professional counselors but by teachers and administrators. This occurs especially in relation to registration advisement, planning of educational activities, and referrals.

need for proficiency

Most continuing education teachers and counselors acquired expertise in subject matter content or counseling procedures before joining the agency. What they typically lack is a detailed understanding of adults as learners and the specific procedures for helping adults learn.

The role of counselor or teacher (as a part time resource person for a continuing education course, workshop, or guided individual study project) tends to be very targeted, unlike most full time teaching in preparatory education which typically deals with a range of courses. In continuing education, the task is typically a specific topic on which the expert will focus during one, five, or ten sessions. If the expert succeeds, it is likely that he or she will be asked to do so again. Otherwise there is usually no ongoing obligation by either agency or expert.

The level and source of skills evinced by instructors successful in continuing education is seldom analyzed. Such differentiation occurs mainly when selecting resource persons or counselors whose ability to effectively help adults learn is uncertain, or when someone who is generally satisfactory in these roles experiences some difficulty.

Resource persons are mainly drawn from two sources, teachers and practitioners. Each can bring distinctive contributions to a continuing education activity, which has implications for staff selection, development, and assignments. Resource persons who are full time teachers and professors will be familiar with formal knowledge of the topic, but may not know about the specific learning tasks it imposes on the adult learner. The other resource persons, usually expert practitioners, may not have formal knowledge and recent research findings.

In continuing education programs, adult participants seek resource persons with expertise in both knowledge and practice. Thus, resource persons who possess both, such as a bank vice president who was formerly a professor of finance or a teacher who had a distinguished career in the performing arts, are especially valuable. Unfortunately, they are rare. As a result, planners seek to staff programs with resource persons whose backgrounds complement each other.

Many of those who work in a counseling capacity have a background as counselors (Riggs, 1978). Some have formal education in basic counseling concepts and procedures. Many informally acquired the ability to establish rapport and facilitate insight and planning. Few devote much time to counseling for major personal adjustment problems, but depend in these instances on specialists. Much of the counselor's time is devoted to advising on the student's role and closely related career and personal plans and coping.

Very few new continuing education teachers and counselors have much preparation in adult development and learning nor in effective procedures to help adults learn. Those with experience in preparatory education are familiar with procedures used there, some of which may be inappropriate for adult learners. Those without such experience often seek very basic information about teaching and counseling procedures (Hansen, Klink, and Kramer, 1973). Because they usually do not view themselves as educators, many are more open to new procedures which help adults learn than those who already view themselves as educators.

There have been a number of studies on the identification of areas of proficiency by those who conduct continuing education activities. Most of them date from the mid 1960s for local extension advisers (Clark, 1960; Gassie, 1965; Metcalfe, 1965; Moore, 1967; Peabody, 1968; Sharma, 1963; Woeste, 1967), and from the late 1960s and early 1970s on workshops for adult basic education teachers (Brooke, 1969; Brown and Dutton, 1972; Dutton and others, 1972; Kincaid and Rink, 1972; Palmer and others, 1969; Rose, 1969). Similar studies have included other categories such as trainers of leaders of youth groups (Stenzel, 1963), teachers aides for new careers programs (Steinberg and Fishman, nd), community college vocational education teachers (Messerschmidt, 1967), and planners of pharmaceutical extension programs (Blockstein and Lemberger, 1966).

areas of proficiency

Two broad areas of proficiency are especially important for continuing education teachers, counselors, and other categories of resource persons. One concerns knowledge of subject matter content and adult development. The second concerns the process of helping adults learn, especially program development procedures (Butcher and LeTarte, 1968; Grabowski, 1976; Sagoff, 1965; Ulmer, 1969). These proficiencies are in addition to the general area of capability that apply to all categories of practitioners. The distinction between knowledge and process seems especially useful in the specification of proficiencies for those who help adults learn. Over the decades, many practitioners have been critical of the overemphasis on knowledge of subject matter and the underemphasis on working effectively with adult learners. A result has been to give major attention to process proficiencies and to downplay the importance of knowledge.

Studies on major areas of proficiency have typically included some on knowledge and some on process. This has occurred for adult basic education teachers (Mocker, 1974; Seaman and others, 1969; Warren, 1966; Zinn, 1974); for local extension advisers (Alexander and Harshaw, 1964; Cook, 1957; Price, 1960; Ussery, 1964); and for resource persons in other continuing education settings such as clergymen (Croft, 1964) and vocational education teachers (Jones, 1967).

Knowledge

Effective instructors, obviously, know much more about the potential use and import of their courses than their students do. An early and important curriculum idea is to state the educational objectives of the course and what the learner should be able to do with it—appreciate, know, perform (Tyler, 1950). This is more likely when the practitioner is familiar with the aspect of adult life in which new learnings are to be applied—for example, a vocational education teacher knows about the jobs in which participants would apply what they learn. Adult learners typically want to apply what they learn to their performance in adult life roles in work, family, and community.

Most continuing education activities focus on fairly specific topics. Usually, various areas of organized knowledge relate to the topic and could be profitably studied. Therefore many of the most effective continuing education activities are multidisciplinary in nature. Experts on the topic should specify course content and make projections regarding desirable new directions for improved performance. Proficient resource persons keep up with major developments in their field and know the educational objectives and clientele background of a specific continuing education activity so that they can emphasize important points as they ask questions, present information, and provide feedback. A discussion leader who is no more knowledgeable about the topic than the students and cannot differentiate an important issue from a trivial one is not likely to be much help when the participants become bogged down in an unimportant point or overlook some fundamental concepts or procedures crucial for their educational progress.

However, possession of high levels of knowledgeability is no guarantee of success when helping adults learn. Most experts achieve their expertise through specialization. Sometimes there are few if any experts available with sufficient breadth of background to enable them to help the adult participants achieve their full range of educational objectives. Under these circumstances there is a tendency to redefine the objectives to fit the available expertise. Where possible, a more satisfactory approach is to include multiple resource persons who collectively can help the participants achieve the educational objectives.

The foregoing uses of knowledgeability have emphasized planning and conducting continuing education activities. This includes both conducting group activities such as courses and workshops, and selecting and preparing learning materials such as prior readings or videotapes. However, knowledgeability is also important in establishing standards of educational progress by participants.

Proficient resource persons use various ways to help participants acquire standards of comparison for their knowledge, performance, and progress by detailed specification of educational needs and objectives which clearly state the desirable knowledge, skills, attitudes, and performance to be achieved. Exemplary adults who have already achieved the objectives can demonstrate how they did so. Feedback and reinforcement help participants identify needed improvement as well as progress achieved. Proficient resource persons do more than help participants find answers for the questions they already have or acquire mastery of procedures for current goals and roles. It is an important part of continuing education to discover new questions and goals.

Proficient continuing education teachers and counselors are also knowledgeable about adult development, as are all categories of practitioners. However, unlike administrators and policy makers, their use of this knowledge about their participants is very closely related to their selection of content and procedures. Thus, one of the crucial areas of proficiency for those who directly help adults to learn has to do with the matching of ideas about content, clients, and procedures. In best practice, this occurs during both the planning and conducting of learning activities.

Program Development

The most important area of proficiency has to do with planning and conducting the teaching-learning transaction (Hansen, Klink, and Kramer, 1973; Mocker, 1974). This process is parallel to program development activities by program administrators, but in this instance involves tasks directly concerned with helping adults learn. The focus of this section is on resource persons, such as teachers and experts, but counselors sometimes relate closely to this process as well. The program development process assumes that resource persons are knowledgeable and use their expertise to take the content into account throughout the process; but they must combine this expertise with an understanding of adult learners and of effective instructional procedures. Although there is a range of important specific proficiencies for continuing education resource persons, they are grouped for illustrative purposes within the five components of the mentor role: needs, context, objectives, activities, and evaluation.

Needs. A proficient resource person tends to be learner oriented. This orientation entails understanding and empathy for the backgrounds and aspirations of the participants and using it in the selection of objectives, content, and learning activities. For some programs, such as adult basic education, this applies especially to minority and ethnic groups of undereducated adults so that programs can be adapted to meet their needs.

Adults engage in continuing education activities for various reasons. In addition to interest in content and in interaction with other participants, the major reason is to achieve a goal or solve a problem related to the participant's adult life roles. An effective resource person is able to use a variety of efficient needs assessment procedures to identify the major gaps between current and desired proficiency by the learners, as perceived by the participants as well as by experts (including the resource person). Illustrative procedures include asking potential participants to identify ways in which they want to become more effective, generalizing from the actual achievements of similar adult learners, and inferring educational needs from evidence of unsatisfactory performance in work, family, or community. Evaluations from previous similar programs can also yield useful insights regarding educational needs and new program ideas. Practitioners tend to be most confident about the validity of needs that emerge from two or more of these sources.

The process of understanding the educational needs and aspirations of participants can be aided by familiarity with generalizations about adult development and learning important for all categories of practitioners. This includes an appreciation of the variety of reasons for adult attendance, the strong interest in application, the impact of change events on their lives, the influence of educational level, the competing priorities from adult responsibilities, and the wish to participate in program decisions. There are additional useful generalizations. One is that increasing experience during adulthood is organized around one's life concerns and contributes to a widening range of individual differences from other adults. Particularly for adults who have not used study skills for a long time, there is an uncertainty about learning ability. Especially during initial sessions it is important to establish an accepting atmosphere and proceed from clarification of expectations and familiar concepts to more challenging ideas (Knowles, 1970; Knox, 1976).

In practice, most continuing education resource persons lack familiarity with generalizations about adult development and learning and fail to identify the most salient characteristics and motives for a specific group of adult learners. Moreover, unfamiliarity with efficient needs assessment procedures causes most resource persons to rely on assumptions, general impressions, and summary information provided by a program administrator. In addition to instructional procedures and materials, a better understanding of clientele needs can be used for planning effective marketing and counseling activities. Also, such activities can in turn yield useful information about client needs.

Context. Effective resource persons consider more than learner needs when setting educational objectives. Many of these other considerations relate to the societal context in which participants function and the organizational context of the agency. Proficient resource persons understand major societal trends and influences which affect program participants in the generation of educational needs and the application of new learnings. An example is shifting employment trends for a vocational education program for adults. The ability to readily identify salient features of the societal context of learners enable a resource person to understand some of the main facilitators and barriers to change. This is especially important in organization development and community development activities. An example is the organization development specialist who recognizes that technological developments are encouraging changed practices but supervisors are discouraging them.

Another benefit of understanding the context is that resource persons can more readily identify and utilize resources within the agency, parent organization, and service area. For example, an art instructor with this proficiency can draw from the experience and expertise of some of the program participants, from library resources in the parent organization, and from exhibits in the community. Taking these and agency purposes into account can enable instructors to provide richer learning experiences than would be likely if they only responded to preferences of the participants.

In practice, many continuing education resource persons rely heavily on their own knowledge of content and awareness of instructional resources, and give scant attention to the ways and settings in which participants are likely to use what they learn. By drawing more from the adult participants themselves, and on their awareness of their educational needs and intended uses of what they learn, proficient resource persons can make continuing education programs more relevant and impactful on performance. Greater understanding of contextual influences can help a resource person recognize constraints that might be alleviated. Examples include time conflicts, inability to pay, and transportation or child care problems. A handbook of related services and resources might enable some teachers and counselors to make referrals and use community resources they might otherwise overlook. Sometimes valuable but underutilized resources exist right in the agency. Pracitioners who are alert to their context can help develop a facilitative and supportive climate for staff as well as participants.

Objectives. Proficient resource persons realize that effective adult learning entails an active search for meaning. Adults usually have substantial experience related to the topics they study, which affects their perceptions in facilitative or in interfering ways. The large amount of new information which confronts adult learners in a continuing education program in addition to what they already know can easily be overwhelming. This is part of the reason why few adults learn, remember, and use answers for which they do not already have the question. Effective resource persons help participants clarify major questions (and what they already know about those questions) before proceeding to present answers.

The ability of adult learners to attend to questions or answers is affected by their adjustment to the learning situation. This is especially important for adults who have been away from formal learning activities for some years and are unfamiliar with procedures such as use of the library, note taking, or preparation of papers. The effective resource person gives special attention to such matters during the initial sessions, to assure that participants feel welcome and oriented to the program and learn something worthwhile.

Proficient resource persons use various procedures to achieve consensus with the participants regarding high priority objectives. Before the program, a planning committee that includes some representative potential participants can consider potential objectives based on information about needs, context, and agency purposes, and select those that seem to have the highest priority. In that priority setting process, proficient resource persons use their content expertise to suggest priorities, but are also attentive to learner concerns about relevance and applications. At an initial session, and at several points throughout a course or workshop, an effective resource person can engage in agenda building with the participants to achieve and maintain consensus on high priority objectives. Even the statement of objectives can emphasize desirable learner knowledge, skills, attitudes, and performance as a result of the educational activity.

In practice, those resource persons who are invited to continue have been fairly responsive to such priorities: Since participation in most continuing education activities is voluntary, it ceases if resource persons are not responsive. In continuing education activities such as conferences and workshops in which there are usually planning committees and multiple resource persons, consensus with participants on high priority objectives is fairly widespread. It may be more difficult for participants and program administrators to agree on important objectives when an instructor conducts a course for adults similar to one he or she conducts as part of a preparatory education program.

Activities. Differences in educational objectives and participant backgrounds and interests make it important that resource persons use a variety of learning activities. Proficient resource persons are able to individualize learning activities to some extent through allowing learners to proceed at their preferred pace as well as to select preferable learning activities so as to fit their learning style.

The appropriateness of the learning activity also relates to the interpersonal setting in which it will occur, such as individual coaching or correspondence study for the individual setting, case analysis, buzz groups, or role playing for the temporary group setting, and team building or conflict resolution activities in organization and community development settings (Bergevin, Morris, and Smith, 1963; Miller, 1964; Rogers, 1971). Proficient resource persons consider the setting and also select learning activities which will enable participants to learn from each other. It is partly because of this that many of the most proficient continuing education resource persons are very effective discussion leaders.

Effective resource persons are able to create memorable encounters. The ways they do so vary greatly. Some rely on persuasive presentations, some use dramatic visual aids, some emphasize participants and guests as role models. Memorable encounters can underscore major concepts and also complement the rehearsal and reinforcement upon which learning depends. Effective activities and materials encourage participants to practice and review which contributes to growing self-confidence and self-recognition as a proficient learner. Another way to highlight major points is to minimize irrelevant and distracting information that tends to interfere with learning, especially by older adults and slow learners.

Proficient resource persons have established criteria for learning activities. Examples include appropriateness for objectives, suitability for learners, effectiveness for the stage of the program, satisfactoriness regarding pacing and variety, and compatibility with their own teaching style. Effective resource persons also realize that successful educational programs have a beginning, middle, and end. Criteria for organizing sequences of learning activities include variety and stage of program, covering major areas of subject matter, continuity without needless overlap, and sequencing so that early parts of the program provide content upon which subsequent parts can build to achieve depth (Knowles, 1970; Knox, 1974).

In practice, teaching style (the basis on which learning activities are selected and organized as well as teaching performance) tends to be very intuitive, to reflect earlier role models, and to include only a limited range of learning activities and planning. With the great range of types of learning activities available, it is appalling that so many resource persons use only a few instructional methods. This is especially the case in those segments of the field which depend mainly on presentation of information by experts and make little use of methods allowing more active participation by learners.

Evaluation. Proficient resource persons develop ways to make judgments based on evidence about the worth and effectiveness of their courses or workshops, and to use the conclusions for program improvement and justification. They also can obtain and use such judgments made by others such as learners, peers, and administrators. Major evaluation activities include planning, selecting, describing, judging, and reporting. One of the stumbling blocks for less proficient teachers of adults is the lack of instruments and procedures for collection of evidence upon which to base descriptions and judgments. Some teachers develop their own tests and normative information for interpretation. Effective resource persons seek out and modify instruments developed by others, as well as develop their own.

Part of evaluation expertise consists of a strategy for selectively engaging in evaluation activities so that the benefits exceed the costs. Data on participant expectations and satisfaction or on follow-up studies regarding application of new learnings can be very helpful. It is often useful to distinguish between formative evaluation of planning and improvement by learners as well as resource persons (such as ongoing evaluation during a weeklong workshop) and summative evaluation of results (such as an external review to decide whether or not to continue a course). Another useful datum is information about expected versus actual performance to show if, when, and where improvement has—or has not—occurred. Information could be collected from participants, teachers, and administrators.

In practice, resource persons who are teachers in preparatory education programs tend to equate evaluation with examining and grading students while other resource persons tend to assume that this type of evaluation is not required in non-credit continuing education programs. As a result learners lack evaluation feedback for how much progress they actually are making. The seemingly complex and technical nature of evaluation tends to intimidate many people who help adults learn, with the result that informal evaluation procedures and findings are underutilized as well as formal evaluation procedures avoided. Rates of attendance and attrition tend to be widely used to judge teacher effectiveness. Program administrators could contribute greatly to constructive evaluation by disseminating examples of effective evaluation instruments.

increasing proficiency

In practice, many persons who serve as resource persons, teachers, and counselors in continuing education programs receive little assistance in becoming more proficient. This is especially so for those who conduct programs on a part and short term basis. The emphasis by program administrators has been on selection of experts who are already well prepared and to continue to use only those who perform well. Furthermore, the part and short term arrangements make staff development difficult. In institutions where administrators in the preparatory education program control the selection of faculty to teach credit courses in the evening or off campus, many continuing education administrators hesitate at trying to increase instructor proficiency.

However, some continuing education agencies do help teachers and counselors increase their proficiency, and such examples could be emulated elsewhere. One of the most extensive efforts to increase the proficiency of those who plan and conduct educational programs for adults occurs in the Cooperative Extension Service of the land grant universities. This partly reflects a long established program with stable funding and full time professional personnel. Staff development activities vary from state to state, but the following practices are quite widespread.

When county extension advisers are hired they undergo a week or more of orientation regarding job duties and university resources. Each year all advisers from around the state are invited to one or more in-service programs held at the university for a week or more, and to local or regional programs for at least a day every month. Extension specialists from the university subject matter departments conduct programs on new developments in their field. In many states, there is a master's degree program in extension education or its equivalent which mainly serves as in-service education for Cooperative Extension Service personnel.

Furthermore, full time advisers typically work with many volunteers and paraprofessional aides (especially in home economics and youth work) to increase their proficiency. Many advisers and specialists themselves are active in professional associations and attend outside courses and workshops which contribute to their expertise.

An increasing number of community colleges have established staff development activities for part time instructors who teach adults. An example is a Saturday workshop on adult learners. Some community colleges have provided teacher orientation programs and organization development projects with increased effectiveness in teaching adults as one major objective.

In some states, regional centers have been established to provide staff development activities for public school teachers of adult education activities. Offering course credit for such activities is an incentive. As with extension advisers, associations for public school adult education teachers also provide programs aimed at increased proficiency. Some university continuing education divisions use a combination of weekend retreats, luncheon meetings, and faculty handbooks for regular faculty members and part time instructors who teach adults in evening or off campus credit courses.

Agencies associated with employers, labor unions, religious institutions, and training adult leaders for youth groups sometimes hold meetings for people who conduct educational programs. These meetings offer presentations and materials with suggestions on effective teaching procedures. There is usually also an opportunity for those who attend to exchange information about experiences and concerns. These meetings usually reflect the fact that most members do not view themselves as mainly teachers and thus tend to be eager to find out what they assume teachers already know about the process of teaching. Some libraries and other providers of book-based discussion groups for adults, such as Great Books, provide leadership training sessions for discussion leaders.

The tradition of supervised clinical experience and critique of performance as part of counselor preparation is reflected in some of the ways used to increase proficiency. Especially in agencies in which there are two or more counselors, informal discussion among members of the counseling staff can help the less experienced counselors in particular discover (1) effective procedures to facilitate the counseling process; (2) useful information sources; (3) helpful contacts for referrals; and (4) beneficial approaches to advocacy.

As continuing education is becoming more widespread and visible, more and more teachers and counselors are acquiring some informal orientation toward helping adults learn even before they first do so through an agency. Many are aware of continuing education activities through the mass media. Articles and even special issues in their professional journals are being devoted to adult development and to continuing education. Some teachers and counselors engaged in graduate study in their own field take one or two courses on adult development or continuing education. The result is a far more receptive approach to efforts to increase proficiency to help adults learn.

The foregoing ways to increase the proficiency of teachers and counselors serve to augment the striving of conscientious agency staff members to become more effective. Some read books and articles and attend meetings to learn more about procedures to facilitate adult learning. However, practitioners and agencies should increase their efforts to augment the proficiency of teachers and counselors, given the difficulty and importance of their roles. Agency program administrators are in a strategic position to assist the resource persons with whom they work in program planning. A valuable by-product of program development can be staff development if program administrators approach their roles in this way.

There are various ways in which program administrators can do so. They can alert resource persons to especially relevant reading materials and meetings that would contribute to their proficiency. They can approach the program development process in ways that help resource persons internalize useful concepts and procedures. They can use program evaluation findings for discussion with resource persons and exploration of improved procedures. They can arrange for talented resource persons who lack experience in adult education to work closely with outstanding practitioners who can serve as role models. One advantage of such activities is that resource persons do not have to travel away from home to participate.

In spite of some effective staff development activities and specific suggestions for improvement, the fundamental discrepancy between the actual and the desirable proficiency of continuing education teachers and counselors arises from the lack of systematic effort toward improvement. Continuing education administrators have mainly depended on selection and retention of part time resource persons to assure quality. An understanding of important areas of proficiency along with effective procedures to increase it can enable resource persons and program administrators alike to diagnose and improve unsatisfactory performance in a targeted and systematic way. For example, orientation sessions can cover clientele characteristics and expectations, interactive instructional methods, and available resources and services.

future directions

There are at least three ways in which progress might be made. One is direct action by continuing education practitioners. A second is by policy making, and a third is by research to produce tested knowledge useful for action or policy making. This concluding section of the chapter suggests desirable future directions for these three types of effort.

Direct Action

One desirable action would be to explore (with representative practitioners and scholars in the field) the extent of consensus regarding major areas of proficiency for continuing education resource persons. This chapter describes some areas which a little supporting literature and much subjective judgment suggests as important. But how much agreement is there on these, and what important areas have been left out?

A second desirable action would be for program administrators to provide summary information about adult development and learning in a form useful for resource persons: Specific generalizations, their relative importance, and the most effective means to communicate them are likely to vary among categories of resource persons. Moreover, program administrators should work with resource persons to help them relate such generalizations to improved practice in helping adults learn.

A third desirable action would be to disseminate information regarding the other areas of proficiency shared by all continuing education practitioners—an understanding of the field and personal qualities such as positive attitudes toward lifelong learning, effective interpersonal relations, and innovativeness. This can help alert resource persons to important proficiencies.

A fourth desirable action would be to encourage program administrators to use a list of desirable proficiencies for resource persons to seek out people from various sources who are very able, and to help them increase certain proficiencies if needed. There is a tendency to draw from established talent pools and to overlook potential resource persons who could make an outstanding contribution.

Resource persons' performance in the teaching-learning transaction is crucial to the success of the entire agency. Thus, a fifth action would be to increase the use of learning activities in which participants are more actively involved in the process, especially the use of methods and materials that do not require extreme amounts of time and money for preparation.

Several desirable actions relate to evaluation. A sixth would be to disseminate criteria and procedures for evaluation of the effectiveness of resource persons in planning and conducting educational programs for adults. A list of proficiencies could serve as a starting point for the criteria. A seventh action related to evaluation would be to develop and disseminate valid and efficient evaluation instruments for which there is a rationale and normative information. In the few instances in which this has occurred, the instruments have been widely used.

The eighth suggested action is for practitioners to share their experience of trying to increase the proficiency of resource persons across segments of the field of continuing education. In the past many useful practices have emerged in one segment of the field (such as training programs by employers, Great Books discussion groups, adult basic education, or Cooperative Extension Service) but diffusion to other segments of the field has been slow. Information about procedures to enable resource persons to become more effective in helping adults learn would appear to be of great interest and applicability across the field.

Policy Questions

There are several policy questions related to proficiencies of resource persons that could be profitably considered by continuing education practitioners. For instance: How can we achieve and preserve a desirable mix of highly proficient resource persons in continuing education? Potential sources include teachers and other experts, both those already associated with the parent organization and those from outside. Over the years, continuing education agencies have drawn moderately from all four of these sources. In recent years, however, restrictions of sources due to organizational circumstances (such as declining enrollments in educational institutions) are occurring during a period when program requirements seem to call for a more varied blend. For example, some employers are expanding the proportion of educational programs for employees conducted internally by the education and training department with use of personnel from the parent organization as resource persons. Some educational institutions with decreasing enrollments and increasingly active teachers' organizations are including in the work agreements first refusal options for full time faculty members regarding teaching in the continuing education programs. Such policies could adversely affect staffing and the proficiency level of resource persons as well as the ability of agencies to select the most able resource persons for short term commitments.

The second policy question relates even more closely to agencies associated with educational institutions, especially in higher education. What will be the relative incentives and rewards to faculty members for effectively helping adults learn? This question is connected with the action step noted earlier regarding criteria and procedures for judging the excellence of faculty performance in conducting continuing education activities. Such criteria are beginning to emerge in some instances. They provide the basis for evidence and judgments so that the quality of performance can be recognized and rewarded. However, there are broader organizational influences related to values and procedures for governance and promotion that have a major impact on the relative reward faculty members receive for conducting continuing education activities. There are few policy issues of greater importance for continuing higher education administrators.

Research

The remaining form of progress toward increased proficiency by continuing education resource persons is research. There are many studies that are needed on this topic (Knox, 1977b). Following are four illustrative research questions. (1) How important for the actual performance of various categories of continuing education resource persons are the areas of proficiency that have thus far been identified? (2) What is the relative effectiveness of various procedures in the attraction and selection of continuing education resource persons? (3) What is the relative effectiveness (regarding learning achievement, persistence in the program, and changed performance) of various types of learning activities? (4) In what ways can program administrators be especially effective in helping resource persons to become more proficient? Conclusions from these and other research questions related to proficiencies of resource persons can produce tested knowledge useful for action and policy making. Practitioners as well as researchers have much to contribute in initiating, planning, and conducting such research, and especially in the utilization of findings.

summary

Resource persons in continuing education are mainly engaged in helping adults learn. Most of them do so on a part time basis as teachers and counselors. Some teachers of adults are regularly teachers in the preparatory education program of schools and colleges. However, the majority of those who help adults learn are regularly practitioners in the fields in which they teach adults. In addition to the few full time professional counselors in continuing education, most of those who help perform the counseling function are teachers and administrators. Very few new continuing education teachers and counselors have much preparation to help adults learn.

Two broad areas of proficiency for resource persons are subject matter knowledgeability and command of program development procedures. In addition to knowing more about concepts and tasks than the typical learner, the resource person should also be familiar with the aspect of adult life in which new learnings are to be applied. A related consideration is an appreciation of multidisciplinary contributions. Knowledgeability is useful in emphasizing important points when planning and conducting continuing education activities. Proficient resource persons are also able to help participants acquire standards of comparison for their knowledge, performance, and progress; to match ideas about content, clients, and procedures; and to deal responsively with specific persons and groups.

The process of planning and conducting effective learning activities for adults entails attention to five components of the mentor role: needs, context, objectives, activities, and evaluation. Use of needs assessment procedures enables the learner oriented resource person to validly identify important educational needs by drawing upon two or more sources. In addition to needs, effective resource persons consider the societal and organizational context regarding agency purposes, resources, community, and influences on participation and application. Proficient resource persons use various procedures to achieve consensus with the participants regarding high priority objectives. Effective resource persons are able to create memorable encounters and individualize learning activities. Criteria for selection of learning activities include appropriateness of objectives, suitability for learners, effectiveness for the stage of the program, satisfactoriness regarding pacing and variety, and compatibility with their own teaching style. Criteria for organizing learning activities include attention to variety and stage of program, covering major areas of subject matter, continuity without needless overlap, and sequencing so that early parts of the program provide prerequisite content upon which subsequent parts can built to achieve depth. Proficient resource persons use program evaluation procedures to make judgments based on evidence about the worth and effectiveness of their programs in ways that encourage use of conclusions for program improvement and justification.

Although in practice resource persons receive little assistance to become more proficient, there are many ways in which they and program administrators can do so. Included are: self-directed study by resource persons, use of planning procedures by program administrators that enhance the proficiency of resource persons, and staff and organization development activities.

The next chapter explores major areas of proficiency that are desirable for those who make or influence the policies and priorities of continuing education agencies.

Those who make policies and decisions that affect continuing education need to understand desirable directions and agency directors can contribute to this process.

policy makers

In addition to agency staff members (such as full and part time administrators, teachers, counselors, and support staff members) there is a broad category of people external to the agency who can influence its functioning for good or ill. Their roles are diverse. What they have in common is that they make decisions and policies that affect continuing education. If they understand and are committed to the continuing education function, their decisions can be supportive and constructive. If not, their resultant policies can intentionally or inadvertently be dysfunctional. One concern of highly proficient agency directors is the proficiency of related policy makers. Therefore, this chapter deals with contributions by both administrators and policy makers to increase the capabilty of policy makers.

The specific proficiencies that are desirable for policy makers, and the types of impact that various levels of proficiency can have on the agency, vary with specific roles of policy makers and with type of agency. The main roles are: administrators elsewhere in the parent organization; policy board members for the agency and/or the parent organization; local, state and federal government administrators; philanthropic officials; local, state and federal legislators; members of state and regional licensing and regulatory agencies; leaders of occupational associations; and administrators of related community organizations and co-sponsors. They all would benefit from at least some understanding and commitment related to the three areas of proficiency common to all practitioners in the field—an understanding of the field and of adults as learners, and perhaps to a lesser extent some of the personal qualities described earlier (Broschart, 1977; Faure, 1972; Lowe, 1975). These general proficiencies along with the specific proficiencies described below help them to make sound decisions regarding rules and resource allocations. The rules include legislation, parent organization policies, and restrictions established by regulatory agencies and associations. The resource allocations include time of resource persons, continuing support, venture capital, and project funds.

areas of proficiency

In practice, most policy makers over the years have been largely unaware of continuing education. With the virtual invisibility of the field until recently, and with their usual concern about competing priorities, policy makers' main contribution (with several notable exceptions) has been benign neglect until recent years. Most policy makers have an area of proficiency that is of value to continuing education administrators. That proficiency is an understanding of the resources and expectations of the organization with which they are associated as these priorities are related to continuing education of adults (Aker and Hanberry, 1972; Aker and Schroeder, 1970). This understanding, along with a familiarity with the way in which the organization functions and decisions are made can enable administrators to more effectively provide information useful to policy makers who make decisions related to continuing education, and to obtain information valuable for agency planning (Bender, 1977; Evans, 1970; Gladieux and Wolanin, 1978; Griffith, 1976; House, 1974; Kerr, 1976; Mann, 1975; Mayhew and Ford, 1974; Wirt, 1975). Outside organizations that sometimes make policies related to continuing education vary greatly in the amount, type, and form of information they provide regarding continuing education. For example, federal government agencies often publish guidelines for the submission and review of grant applications, but private philanthropic foundations seldom do. State regulatory agencies and governing boards, along with regional accrediting associations, often have printed guidelines for approval of new program requests, but this is seldom the case for administrators in the parent organization, or members of policy boards or relevant legislative committees. When guidelines and procedures are mainly oral instead of written it is doubly important that continuing education administrators understand and enhance the proficiency levels of policy makers.

As indicated earlier, desirable proficiencies vary with policy making roles. Administrators elsewhere in the parent organization should understand major interrelationships between the continuing education function and other functions of the parent organization (Penfield, 1975). This is especially important for the administrator to whom the director of the continuing education agency reports, but it is also important for other members of the central administration of the parent organization and for administrators in various parts of the organization who participate in decision making related to continuing education. This understanding of interrelationships includes not only the resources (such as money, personnel, use of facilities) which the agency would like to obtain from the parent organization but also the ways in which the continuing education function contributes to the achievement of organizational goals, to increased support for the organization, and to the effectiveness of other parts of the organization. For an agency located in an educational institution such interrelationships might include an understanding of major ways in which individuals and organizations in the service area benefit from continuing education, what this contributes to institutional support, and how faculty contributions to conducting continuing education activities for adults can also contribute to faculty understanding of current issues and procedures of concern to the adult participants. This can enrich scholarship and teaching of full time students in the preparatory education program. For an employer's training and education department, such interrelationships include an understanding of major ways in which staff and organization development activities contribute to improved communication and team building, increased productivity of sales or service, and reduced accidents or absenteeism (Hackman and others, 1975; Miles, 1965).

For members of the policy board of the agency and/or parent organization, important proficiencies include both an understanding of agency resources, activities, and accomplishments, and a sense of likely future directions. With the turnover of the membership of most policy boards, their part time commitment to the role, and the variety of other policy issues they typically confront, briefings and up-dates are an unending task for an agency director who seeks responsive policy making. The dynamics are somewhat different for members of a policy board exclusively for the agency (in contrast with the general policy board for the total parent organization, such as the school board, the company board of directors, the college or library trustees, or the association board of directors). Most continuing education agencies do not have a separate policy board. Exceptions include the Cooperative Extension Service county advisory committee, the professional association education committee, and the school or community college citizens advisory committee (Kogan and Packwood, 1974). For such agency connected policy boards, the members typically bring with them some background and commitment regarding continuing education. In addition to contributions to policy making for the agency, it is usually expected that the members will give advice regarding client needs and other matters and help interpret agency goals and programs to people in the service area.

As agency directors consider current and desirable proficiencies of policy board members for purposes of selection and orientation it is important to consider *both* directions in the flow of information to and from the service area. For general policy boards of the parent organization, orientation to the continuing education function is a major consideration. Efforts to increase proficiency more often depend on other administrators in the central administration of the parent organization who mainly deal with the policy board. An important proficiency is an appreciation of major benefits and activities of continuing education which should be helped by new policies or at least not inadvertantly harmed by other policy decisions. These types of understandings and commitments are best advanced by persons other than the continuing education director and before a crisis occurs.

Administrators of government agencies related to continuing education may perform several relevant roles. One is to disperse funds and monitor programs and expenditures as provided under legislation. Examples include federal funds for the Cooperative Extension Service from the Smith Lever Act of 1914, for adult basic education from amendments to Title III of the Elementary and Secondary Education Act of 1965 (amended in 1974) and for vocational education for adults from the Vocational Education Act of 1965. In many instances, such formula funds are allocated to states so most of a director's contact is with a state agency, except for discretionary funds for special projects or research which are sometimes allocated from federal or regional levels. Most such public funds are for agencies associated with public institutions, but some government grant programs are available to private non-profit organizations (such as in the arts and humanities) and to employers and labor unions (such as in vocational education). In some instances, such as the Comprehensive Employment and Training Act of 1973, refunding is handled through local or regional prime contractors (Christoffel, 1978; Griffith, 1976; Houle, 1968).

Another governmental agency role is encouraging innovation. This occurs as guidelines change, and as special funding is provided for research, for staff development, for demonstration projects, and for innovative activities. An important proficiency for governmental officials has to do with an understanding of interrelationships between stability and change along with the constructive contributions that can be made by provider agencies and by government agencies. A related proficiency is an appreciation of especially effective current projects and of promising future directions (Broschart, 1977). Practitioners in local agencies can help to provide this type of information; if they are successful, they are a major beneficiary. So many governmental activities contribute to stability or disruption, that a concerted effort by government officials and practitioners in the field to achieve some desired changes can be beneficial for all concerned.

Foundation officials can make contributions similar to government officials who administer grant programs, but their method of operation is usually quite different. Because the philanthropic foundation makes grants for the initiation of deserving projects but does not perform most of the other functions of government agencies such as monitoring, their contribution to continuing education can be somewhat distinctive. Without many contacts within the field other than grant support for projects, foundation officials emphasize project results and personalized application and review procedures, while many government granting agencies emphasize detailed guidelines and application forms. These characteristics contribute to a desirable proficiency by foundation officials—the ability to recognize promising ideas, capable personnel, and funding patterns likely to help launch projects with a lasting impact. Continuing education practitioners who prepare proposals might consider ways to enhance this proficiency. Experience in a foundation or government agency can also provide a vantage point from which to identify general issues. It would seem desirable to find ways to share these insights more broadly with practitioners in the field.

Legislators are perhaps least likely to recognize their connection with the field of continuing education. However, they and their staff members have and can contribute enormously to policy making and priority setting

(Christoffel, 1978; Gladieux and Wolanin, 1978; Griffith, 1976). Especially in serving harder to reach adults, legislative appropriations have been quite influential. A few legislators have had prior contact with continuing education or related activities which contributed to their understanding and commitment. However, the short tenure of most legislators and the wide variety of issues with which they deal makes it somewhat difficult to enhance their proficiency in continuing education. Constituents who appreciate its benefits can be effective advocates and their staff members can be effective allies. One very useful effort would be programs for members of legislative staff on the topic of continuing education. If legislators are to support proposals for continuing education, they must be convinced that such legislation would be of greater benefit for more people than competing proposals. Practitioners who seek to obtain legislation for continuing education will require both a persuasive rationale and familiarity with the actual process by which legislation is proposed and enacted.

As continuing education is becoming more prominent, there are more people associated with occupational associations, licensing and regulatory agencies, and accrediting associations who help to set policies related to continuing education. This role is illustrated by the emergence of continuing education activity as a requirement for recertification and relicensure of professionals. In many fields, some members of the professional association are active in the process of licensing, registration, and certification. Initiatives related to continuing education may come from regulatory agencies, from associations, or a combination of the two. People who perform these roles can benefit from an understanding of the likely contribution of continuing education participation to increased proficiency, in contrast with the usual focus on protection of the public from practitioners who engage in sub-standard practice. Another desirable proficiency is an understanding of the characteristics of effective continuing education programs that can be used when approving or accrediting programs.

Many continuing education directors work with administrators of related community organizations and co-sponsors. Examples include employment and welfare offices which sometimes refer clients to continuing education agencies, or employers who co-sponsor such programs for their employees at the place of work. Although such administrators do not formally make policies for a continuing education agency, they can influence the program by their own policies and practices. Administrators of these related organizations can be more effective if they are generally familiar with the continuing education agency, are able to promote interagency cooperation, and are convinced that the benefits of collaboration are worth the costs.

increasing proficiency

There are various ways in which those who make or influence policies related to continuing education can increase their proficiency to do so. Practitioners can assist in the process. The preceding section on Areas of Proficiency of policy makers deals with the continuing education function. However, it might be helpful to review the range of ways in which this might be accomplished because many might be relevant in a specific instance.

Perhaps the most effective way to increase the proficiency of policy makers to deal with issues related to continuing education is through personal contact with practitioners in the field. This contact can occur in many settings and even indirectly through intermediaries. The settings include appointments at policy makers' offices, phone conversations or correspondence, and interaction in other organizations to which both the policy maker and the continuing education administrator belong. Examples of indirect contact include working closely with legislative aides, or having beneficiaries of continuing education programs talk with policy board members they happen to know. Common to all of these forms of personal contact is that the policy maker becomes familiar with continuing education programs, results, and issues through interaction with someone who is familiar with specific programs. Some such contacts can be arranged but some of the most effective ones occur because a practitioner was able to seize the opportunity when it arose.

Another way to increase policy maker proficiency regarding continuing education is through meetings of various kinds. Examples include legislative hearings, site visits related to a proposal, presentations at policy board meetings, and administrative staff meetings within the parent organization.

The reporting process can also contribute to proficiency, although it seldom does. Most continuing education agencies prepare more reports than seem necessary. Although they often contain much information relevant to policy makers, they are seldom useful to them. Practitioners who effectively use reports for policy makers keep them short and interesting and include examples of benefits to continuing education participants and the larger society. In addition to regular reports, other types of materials can be used to enhance the proficiency of policy makers. For example, video tapes can dramatically portray activities, participants, and benefits in a way difficult to achieve with a written report. Evaluation and marketing activities of an agency can support the preparation of such reports and materials.

As indicated earlier, preparing and evaluating proposals can provide a very effective vehicle for increasing the proficiency of policy makers, especially administrators in the parent organization, policy board members, and officials of funding agencies and foundations.

Paramount among the abilities of continuing education administrators is an active strategy for the identification of policy makers whose increased understanding and commitment related to continuing education is important.

future directions

As continuing education of adults becomes more visible and central in our society and in many types of organizations, the proficiency of policy makers to deal with continuing education issues has become exceedingly important. Continuing education practitioners can no longer depend on benign neglect as an adequate policy framework. In addition, it is increasingly clear that many programs for underserved and less advantaged adults require more formal attention to policy making and financial support. The lack of serious attention to policy making related to continuing education is reflected in the very modest amount of research findings and professional literature available on this topic. It would be desirable to increase the proficiency of policy makers regarding continuing education issues and the mutually beneficial relationships between policy makers and continuing education practitioners. Research and demonstration projects can make important contributions, as can dissemination of reports of experiences by practitioners who have been successful in this regard.

However, the crucial issue regarding policy making and continuing education is how much initiative practitioners take in relation to policy makers. There is a long history of reluctance by educators of all types to become involved in political affairs and policy making (Griffith, 1976). However, circumstances have been changing and continuing education practitioners have more opportunities to relate to policy makers than do many other types of educators. Practitioners who want to do so have the advantage that their profession deals with continuing education of adults; there are many ways in which policy makers can be involved in the process.

Policy makers can be invited as speakers and special guests at meetings of continuing education practitioners and as resource persons at many types of continuing education programs. Programs can also be conducted for policy makers, especially around issues that are of special concern to them. For all these suggestions there is a word of caution. If efforts to increase the proficiency of policy makers are well planned and conducted, it is likely that they will learn something and increase their understanding of and commitment to the field as well. If such activities are poorly conducted the opposite effect is likely. In planning such programs for policy makers it should be remembered that one of the marks of effective continuing education programs is their being planned *with* the participants so as to be responsive to their educational needs.

One of the most influential types of policy makers is the person in the parent organization to whom the agency director reports. Examples include the superindendent of schools for the director of continuing higher education, the academic vice president for the director of continuing higher education, the vice president for personnel for the training director, and the executive director for the staff member who coordinates continuing education activities for a professional association. Agency directors should become more effective in the strategies they use to increase such policy makers' understanding of the continuing education function. Some of the most promising strategies are subsumed in the literature and practice of planned organizational change (Lindquist, 1978). Major procedures for planned change include: identification of unmet needs within the parent organization, location of promising practices that could be readily adapted in response to local needs, use of linkage procedures that provide direct contact between knowledge resources and local persons, open development and decision on change proposals, and support for implementation.

summary

Policy makers make decisions and policies that affect continuing education. They do so as administrators in the parent organization, policy board members, government and foundation administrators, legislators, and leaders of associations and community organizations. Although until recently their main contribution to continuing education has been benign neglect, they are having an increasing impact. The main desirable area of proficiency for policy makers is an adequate knowledge of desirable directions for agency development.

Ways in which policy makers can become more proficient in relation to continuing education include personal contact, meetings, reports, and proposals. As continuing education is becoming a more central societal and organizational concern, continuing education administrators should take the initiative to identify influential policy makers and to help them become more proficient regarding the continuing education function.

For each role and area of proficiency there are desirable future directions regarding direct action, needed policies, and research.

summary and future directions

Much of the vitality and impact of continuing education depends on the proficiency of the practitioners who plan and conduct educational programs for adults who participate on a part time or short term basis. Included as practitioners are administrators, resource persons (teachers, counselors, experts), and policy makers. They work in a wide variety of continuing education agencies that are part of schools, colleges, universities, employers, labor unions, religious institutions, libraries, hospitals, associations, and many types of community organizations.

With the growing size and visibility of the field of continuing education, many people have recently assumed responsibilities as continuing education practitioners. These have shown an increasing interest in the specification of major areas of proficiency. Such an overview of continuing education practitioner proficiency can be useful in several ways, including: identification of major capabilities for practitioners to keep in mind as they strive to become more effective; suggestion of major topics as agencies, associations, and university graduate programs provide educational programs for practitioners; and generation of questions for research regarding practitioner proficiency.

This sourcebook provides such an overview of practitioner proficiency. It discusses concepts from previous studies about what continuing education practitioners should know and be able to do; outlines typical and desirable proficiencies that are shared by all categories of practitioners; and specifies proficiencies that are somewhat distinct for administrators, resource persons, and policy makers. Proficiency is defined as a desirable achievable level of capability to perform, such as could be achieved by most able practitioners. The overview briefly identifies major areas of proficiency and suggests typical and desirable types and levels for each. The experience with competency-based preparatory education indicates some of the difficulties in setting specifications for a proficiency approach to education, but also suggests that it is especially appropriate for those who conduct continuing education for adults.

Three core areas of proficiency appear to benefit all categories of continuing education practitioners. These core proficiencies are an understanding of the field of continuing education, an understanding of adults as learners, and personal qualities such as positive attitudes toward lifelong learning, effective interpersonal relations, and innovativeness. In addition, effective administrators have major proficiencies related to administration, effective program development, and the use of research; resource persons have major proficiencies related to knowledgeability and the process of helping adults learn; and effective policy makers have major proficiencies related to priorities and resources for strengthening the continuing education function.

The focus of most previous studies of practitioner proficiencies has been on administrators and the contribution of graduate study, although there has been some attention to resource persons especially in adult basic education and the Cooperative Extension Service (Aker, 1963; Campbell, 1977; Houle, 1964; Jensen, Liveright, and Hallenbeck, 1964; Knox, 1973; Spear, 1976; Veri, 1968; Verner and others, 1970). Some statements have contributed to a general model of educational program components (Tyler, 1950) and to areas of needed research (Knox, 1977b).

There are various ways in which practitioners can increase their proficiency through informal personal efforts and through participation in more structured educational activities. Included are: remembering and applying what is known and now recognized as pertinent, learning from experience (such as trying a new approach), learning from associates (such as a mentor relationship), learning from people from other places and times (such as reading and attending professional association meetings) and discovering what nobody knows (such as conducting research).

practitioners generally

All categories of practitioners would benefit from three areas of proficiency—a perspective on the field, an understanding of adults as learners, and personal qualities (such as commitment, interpersonal effectiveness, and an innovative approach to practice). Research should discover the relative importance of these areas of proficiency for effective performance by each category of practitioner at various career stages.

A perspective on the field of continuing education includes attention to provider agencies, the parent organization, societal influences, and awareness of resources. In practice, this perspective tends to be fragmentary and to be acquired mainly from experience and contacts in the type of agency with which a practitioner is associated. It seems desirable to help practitioners gain a more comprehensive and useful perspective on the field. This is likely to entail reading and research.

In practice, most practitioners enter their first position with a continuing education agency through a prior association with the parent organization. For example, a vocational education teacher with administrative certification becomes director of public school adult education. Familiarity with the agency and similar continuing education agencies tends to result from experience and contact with associates. However, some agencies are parts of educational institutions and some are parts of other types of parent organizations such as employers, labor unions, religious institutions, professional associations, and all types of community organizations. Most practitioners associate with others from agencies similar to their own and perhaps one or two other types that co-sponsor programs. Practitioners with a broad perspective on many types of providers typically gain it from reading books and journals, and from participation in meetings, courses, and workshops which include information and people from various segments of the field.

Relationships between the continuing education agency and the rest of the parent organization are crucial for most practitioners. In practice, practitioners learn to understand and deal with these relationships from experience, although some attention is given to them in professional association meetings and publications. The literature on agency functioning and organizational behavior can contribute greatly to a practitioner's understanding and effectiveness (Bennis and others, 1976; Carey, 1963; Clark, 1956; Cohen and March, 1974; Daigneault, 1963; Darkenwald, 1977; Farmer and Knox, 1977; Katz and Kahn, 1966; Knox, 1975; Mezirow, Darkenwald, and Knox, 1975; Schein, 1978; Shaw, 1969; Smith, Aker, and Kidd, 1970).

It is difficult for most practitioners to obtain a very detailed understanding of societal influences without reading in the professional literature to learn about people from other places and times. This literature includes attention to past and future trends (Grattan, 1971; Knowles, 1977) as well as issues (Apps, 1973; Blakely and Lappin, 1969; Broschart, 1977; Ziegler, 1970).

A perspective on the field also includes an awareness of resources such as professional literature and sources of financial support. In practice, some practitioners discover valuable resources in the process of preparing proposals for new programs. In addition, directories and inventories of resources can make a valuable contribution if practitioners know about them (Niemi and Jessen, 1976).

A desirable course of action for enlarging a practitioner's perspective on the field would be greater effort by agencies and professional associations in helping them to do so through reading and contact with colleagues in other segments of the field. Research should be conducted on which aspects of such a perspective are most salient for each category of practitioners, and on the most effective ways to help practitioners gain such a perspective.

An understanding of adult development and learning is important to all categories of practitioners because it helps explain personal and situational influences on the decision to participate, circumstances under which adults with various characteristics learn most effectively, and influences on the application and use of new learnings. Most practitioners acquire their understanding of adults as learners through personal and agency experience. In recent years, the rapidly expanding research literature on adult development and learning has been summarized and made more accessible to practitioners (Howe, 1977; Knox, 1977a; Schein, 1978; Tough, 1978).

Generalizations about adult development are especially useful to practitioners in relation to role performance, change events, information seeking, and self concept. Generalizations about adult learning are especially useful to practitioners in relation to learning ability, search for meaning, adjustment during learning activity, physical influences, self pacing, interference from misunderstandings, importance of reinforcement, and effectiveness of feedback.

A detailed understanding from reading about developmental trends and mechanisms can enable practitioners to gain greater insight and empathy regarding the specific adults with whom they work. Such understanding can be especially useful for needs assessment, marketing, preparation and selection of relevant educational materials, and priority setting.

Research should be conducted on the aspects of adult development and learning that are most salient for each category of practitioners, and on the most effective ways to help practitioners gain and use such understandings. Particular attention should be given to practitioner's use of generalizations from the literature in order to learn more about specific clients from experience and associates.

Important personal qualities of effective practitioners include commitment, interpersonal effectiveness, and approach to practice. Professional values include a commitment to the broad field of continuing education in addition to the primary allegiance that most practitioners have to their type of agency. The latter grows out of day to day professional obligations and aspirations, the former requires deliberate effort. Interpersonal effectiveness includes winning cooperation on which so much of practitioner effectiveness depends. Major aspects of interpersonal effectiveness are typically possessed by practitioners when they enter the field, and this should be recognized in staff recruitment and selection activities. However, the success of educational programs for adults regarding sensitivity, assertiveness, and communication indicates that practitioners can usually become more effective in their interpersonal relations if they want to. An innovative approach to professional practice includes attention to creativity and problem solving (Argyris and Schön, 1976; Bradford, Gibb, and Benne, 1964; Hackman and others, 1975; Houle, 1961; Knox, 1974; Lindquist, 1978; Schein, 1978; Spear, 1976).

As with the other two areas of proficiency that seem to apply to all categories of practitioners, personal qualities are important as they contribute to professional effectiveness in the field as well as in the agency. Research should be conducted on which aspects of these personal qualities are most salient for each category of practitioners, and on the most effective ways to help practitioners gain and use such qualities. Particular attention should be given to the relative contributions of experience, associates, and contact with more formal educational activities that include reading and discussion with people who are not work associates.

administrators

Continuing education administrators include agency directors, program administrators, and persons who perform other specialized administrative and support roles. They have demanding roles with high expectations, limited support, primary reliance on part time resource persons, and limited specialized preparation (Smith, Aker, and Kidd, 1970). There is a substantial literature on opinions about areas of proficiency that continuing education administrators should have, but more research is needed that collects information from various categories of administrators themselves and includes analysis of actual practice. Three important areas of proficiency for continuing education administrators are administration, program development, and research (Knox, forthcoming).

The art and science of administration includes attention to participation, resources, staffing, and leadership (Caplow, 1967; Drucker, 1966; Shaw, 1969). Marketing and counseling activities help to attract and retain adult participants, with an emphasis on client orientation and mutually beneficial exchange (Kotler, 1974). Because most continuing education participation is voluntary and participation rates increase with level of formal education, many practitioners are concerned about ways to reach underserved adults (Boaz, 1978; Johnstone and Rivera, 1965; London, Wenkert and Hagstrom, 1963). Administrators can use available generalizations to better serve harder to reach adults. In addition, research is needed on the relative effectiveness of marketing strategies for various target markets and types of programs. A major policy question is how much are agencies and society willing to devote to subsidy of continuing education for harder to reach and largely undereducated adults?

Administrators devote much of their effort to acquisition and allocation of resources. This includes budgeting, proposal preparation, and obtaining funds for the agency from participants and other sources (Hentschke, 1975). There is a tendency for such activities to displace time for program development; thus one important area of proficiency is to be able to relate activities regarding resources to agency goals and program development activities. A related policy issue has to do with provision of financial assistance to continuing education participants.

Decisions on staff selection and development are crucial to agency success, especially systematic efforts to increase the effectiveness of part time staff who help adults learn (Flippo, 1976; Lindquist, 1978). Highly proficient program administrators use effective program development procedures that encourage staff members to remember and apply what they learn in staff development activities (Spear, 1976).

Administrative leadership entails planning and coordination to facilitate staff satisfaction and productivity (Blake and Mouton, 1964). With the lack of institutionalization of most continuing education agencies, a proficient continuing education administrator can do much to provide direction and stability (Cohen and March, 1974; Katz and Kahn, 1966; Mezirow, Darkenwald, and Knox, 1975). However, innovation and priority setting can be difficult from the power poor position that most continuing education administrators occupy (Darkenwald, 1977; Farmer and Knox, 1977). Effective administrators are able to identify people who are likely to be very influential on continuing education policies and to help them understand the main issues, programs, and clientele groups to which their policies relate. Within the parent organization, procedures for planned organizational change can be very useful (Lindquist, 1978). Practitioners tend to gain a perspective on the entire field through reading, association activities, and graduate study.

In practice, continuing education administrators deal with specific issues and decisions that often relate to aspects of participation, resources, staffing and leadership. An overview of major areas of administrative proficiency can contribute to an administrator's ability to identify relevant readings and topics to discuss with associates.

Effective continuing education administrators give special attention to program development because it is so central to the quality of offerings to adult participants and because without a full time faculty, administrators can readily perform a major program development role (Beckhard, 1969; Bennis, 1969; Havelock, 1969; Miller, 1964; Smith, Aker, and Kidd, 1970). Although the specifics vary with agency and administrative role, planning and conducting an educational program entails five components—needs, context, objectives, activities, and evaluation (Houle, 1972; Knowles, 1970; Knox, 1974; Pennington and Green, 1976).

There are various needs assessment procedures which effective administrators can use to originate new continuing education programs and to modify existing ones so that they are relevant to the clientele. Highly proficient administrators tend to use more formal needs assessment procedures which entail cross validation by use of two or more types of evidence about educational needs (Knox, 1974). Evaluation of pilot projects and opinions by current participants regarding additional programs they would like can also yield useful information for needs assessment. In addition to research on the relative effectiveness of various combinations of needs assessment activities, practitioners should be encouraged to use effective procedures to identify important educational needs that the clientele is ready to pursue.

The context for program development includes resources, facilitators, and barriers in the agency, parent organization, and service area that can contribute to the effectiveness of the continuing education program and to the extent to which participants apply what they learn (Knox, 1974). Examples include outstanding resource persons, sources of financial assistance to participants, purposes of the parent organization, and current job markets. Proficient administrators are able to utilize relevant resources and sources of encouragement and to deflect or compensate for influences that discourage adults from learning and using what they learn.

Objective setting includes selecting and prioritizing intended learner outcomes. Proficient administrators seek to achieve consensus on objectives by learners and resource persons through procedures such as planning committees and agenda building (Knowles, 1970). There is a wide range of learning activities that can be included in a continuing education program (Klevins, 1972; Miller, 1964; Rogers, 1971; Solomon, Bezdek and Rosenberg, 1963). Proficient administrators encourage planners to select activities from throughout that range, with an emphasis on active learner participation, and to organize programs so that they have a beginning, middle, and end. A more explicit awareness of program development components can help administrators learn from their experience and from their associates as well as from reading about program development procedures.

Program evaluation can consist of internal evaluation for program improvement and external evaluation for program justification (Grotelueschen, Gooler, and Knox, 1976; Knox, 1976). Proficient administrators provide leadership regarding evaluation by helping to focus the effort and providing resources, release time, and encouragement to facilitate the conducting of evaluations and use of conclusions. In practice, enrollment trends, attrition rates, financial summaries, participant opinions, and evidence of practice adoption are used in program evaluation. Research should be conducted on the impact of continuing education participation on relevant aspects of adult role performance. Such research can help identify indexes of application which can be feasibly used in the evaluation of impact. Research should also be conducted on the relative effectiveness of general program development strategies used by program administrators as they work with clients and resource persons.

Although continuing education administrators are action oriented, there is an important contribution that many can make to the production and consumption of the growing amount of research regarding continuing education. This research deals with adults as learners, program development, agency functioning, and societal trends and issues. Administrators who are proficient regarding research procedures and findings can contribute to generating questions for research, to facilitating data collection, and to encouraging use of findings.

There are a number of ways in which continuing education administrators can increase their proficiency regarding administration, program development, and research. One way is through interaction with agency tasks and personnel. This could occur through informal but reflective contact with agency staff members, as well as formal staff development activities. A second way is by participation in continuing education association activities, both those related to the administrators' segment of the field to which he or she tends to have the main allegiance, and those associations and publications that span the various segments of the field. A third way is by self-directed study, in which administrators are fairly active but for which supporting materials such as self assessment inventories and study guides are much needed. A fourth way is by participation in courses, workshops, and degree programs conducted by university graduate programs with a specialization in continuing education.

teachers and counselors

The resource persons who help adults learn consist mainly of teachers and counselors. Most of the teachers of adults do so on a part time basis in addition to their main responsibilities as preparatory education teachers or practitioners in a wide variety of fields. Most have no preparation for teaching adults before they first do so. The continuing education counseling function is performed mainly by teachers and administrators, but a few full time counselors have some background in counseling (Farmer, 1971; Knox and Farmer, 1977).

Effective teachers of adults tend to combine subject matter knowledge with a familiarity with how adults use the content in practice, along with a familiarity with the process of helping adults learn. In practice, it is difficult to find resource persons who combine these proficiencies; this leads to using several resource persons in a continuing education activity and to efforts by program administrators to help resource persons become more proficient in planning and conducting effective continuing education activities. There have been some research studies which suggest important areas of proficiency for continuing education resource persons.

Two broad areas of proficiency for resource persons are knowledgeability regarding content and effectiveness in the process of helping adults learn. For counselors, knowledgeability regarding adult development is the counterpart to content mastery for teachers (Heffernan, Macy, and Vickers, 1976). For teachers, an understanding of adult development can contribute to selection of content and of procedures. Administrators can help resource persons to become more proficient in this regard by providing them with summary information about adult development and other background concepts relevant to all categories of practitioners. Much more research and consensus among practitioners is needed regarding important areas of proficiency by continuing education resource persons.

Knowledge of content helps resource persons specify standards for the proficiencies that adult learners seek to achieve. Because the experts who serve as resource persons tend to be specialists in one field while adult learners are typically interested in various problem areas, multidisciplinary programs are often especially appropriate.

Proficiency in the process of helping adults learn entails attention to program development components that parallel those used by program administrators—needs, context, objectives, activities, and evaluation. In practice, experienced resource persons tend to be learner-oriented but to be unfamiliar with detailed generalizations about adult development and learning, and with needs assessment procedures. Program administrators can encourage use of needs assessment procedures such as asking participants, generalizing from achievements of similar adults, and making inferences from unsatisfactory conditions (Knowles, 1970). Resource persons can also be encouraged to analyze the context so as to identify influences and resources that should be taken into account when setting educational objectives and when trying to identify likely constraints on application of new learnings (Houle, 1972). Efforts to help resource persons become more proficient regarding needs and context culminate in objective setting. In addition to emphasizing important objectives, resource persons can be encouraged to use procedures to achieve consensus with the participants regarding objectives.

Effective resource persons select from a range of learning activities and organize them to allow individualization by adult learners to fit preferred pacing and learning style (Biddle and Biddle, 1965; Bradford, Gibb, and Benne, 1964; Craig, 1976; Klevins, 1972; Knowles, 1970; Knox, 1976; Miller, 1964; Rogers, 1971). Proficiency also includes emphasizing major aspects of each topic. Although additional research is needed on the relative effectiveness of various types of learning activities in relation to objectives and learner characteristics, program administrators can use existing knowledge to encourage resource persons to use instructional methods that entail a more active role by participants, such as case discussion (Stenzel and Feeney, 1970).

Proficient teachers of adults use evaluation for program improvement as well as justification. One way to emphasize improvement is to compare expectations with achievement. Program administrators can help plan useful evaluation activities of a manageable scale, and help prepare appropriate evaluation criteria and instruments.

Because of the part time and short term arrangements of most resource persons to help adults learn, administrators have typically relied on selection and selective retention to maintain program quality and have done little to help resource persons increase their proficiency. Exceptions include Cooperative Extension Service local advisers and in recent years adult basic education teachers. The areas of proficiency included in this overview can be used by resource persons interested in striving to become more effective. They can compare these proficiencies with an appraisal of their current proficiencies to identify growth goals. Program administrators can also use this list of proficiencies for staff selection and development. Research is also needed on this topic. Attention should be given to the relative effectiveness of strategies to use proficiency areas in staff selection and development, as well as ways to involve resource persons in program development so as to increase their proficiency. Program administrators should be encouraged to share experiences with colleagues in the field regarding efforts to increase the proficiency of resource persons.

policy makers

Policies affecting the continuing education agency are made by people in a variety of roles. Included are administrators in the parent organization, members of the policy or advisory board, government administrators, foundation officials, legislators, members of regulatory agencies, association leaders, and representatives of co-sponsoring agencies. In practice, many are unaware of continuing education agencies. The main desirable area of proficiency for policy makers is an adequate knowledge of desirable directions for agency development. Policy makers also have areas of competence, such as an understanding of how their organization functions, that can contribute to continuing education administrators as they seek to improve relationships.

The main areas of desirable proficiency vary somewhat among policy making roles. Administrators in the parent organization, such as the person to whom the director reports, should understand interrelationships between the continuing education function and other functions of the parent organization, such as preparatory education or production of goods and services. Members of the policy board should understand current agency activities and desirable future directions (Houle, 1960). Government administrators should understand contributions of the continuing education agency and of government to agency stability and change, along with characteristics of effective agency programs and desirable future directions. Foundation officials should understand the contribution of agency innovation to society and can share with practitioners their perceptions of promising ideas. Legislators should understand the likely benefits of program support, especially in relation to harder to reach adults. Other policy makers, such as those connected with regulatory agencies and professional associations, should understand the likely contribution of continuing education to adult role performance. Representatives of co-sponsors should understand mutually beneficial relationships with continuing education agencies.

There are various ways in which policy makers can become more proficient in relation to continuing education. Agency administrators can help through personal contact and materials. Personal contact can include office visits, phone calls, and correspondence, but also joint participation in meetings and hearings arranged by the continuing education administrator as well as the policy maker. Materials can include reports and proposals that may incorporate concepts from the literature of the field but should be brief, targeted, and dramatize the benefits to society.

As the continuing education function is moving from the margin toward the core of societal and organizational concern, policy makers are becoming increasingly important to continuing education agencies, especially in relation to underserved adults. Continuing education administrators should take the initiative to identify influential policy makers and to help them become more proficient regarding the continuing education function. Fortunately, continuing education provides many opportunities for contact between agency staff and policy makers, including inviting them to serve as speakers and providing education activities planned for them. To achieve the desired result, it is important that such activities be effectively conducted. Research and development projects should be conducted so that the field generally can better understand effective relationships between agencies and policy makers.

conclusion

This sourcebook has provided an overview of major areas of proficiency for continuing education practitioners. Its purpose has been to describe major areas of proficiency that seem important for various categories of practitioners, and to indicate the scope of the field to which the quarterly sourcebook series relates. There are various ways in which practitioners can use this overview: (1) Individual practitioners might use it to identify desirable areas of professional growth. (2) Directors might use the overview to help plan staff recruitment, selection and orientation activities. (3) Agency administrators might use the overview to identify important topics for staff development activities to be conducted by the agency or by professional associations. (4) Directors might use the overview to decide on concepts to convey to policy makers. (5) Professors of continuing education might compare the overview with course offerings in an effort to improve graduate programs as they seek to prepare capable practitioners for the field. (6) Researchers might use the overview to generate research questions about continuing education practitioner proficiency.

The growing size, visibility, and expectations regarding continuing education of adults is creating an unprecedented challenge to continuing education practitioners. How this challenge is met depends mainly on the types and levels of distinctive professional proficiency that practitioners possess. Unless practitioners are able to make distinctive contributions that are not forthcoming from practitioners in related fields, it is likely that much of the continuing education function will be performed elsewhere in parent organizations. This overview suggests major areas of proficiency to be seriously considered by practitioners.

references

Adelson, M. "Creativity and the Third Culture: A University-Level Problem." *UCLA Educator,* 1976, *18* (2), 41-49.

Aker, G. F. *Criteria for Evaluating Graduate Study in Adult Education.* Chicago: Center for Continuing Education, University of Chicago, 1963.

Aker, G. F., and Hanberry, G. C. (Eds.). *Strategies for Decision-Making in Adult Basic Education. Final Report of Phase II of a National Training Institute for State Directors and Other Administrators of Public Adult Education.* Tallahassee: Florida State University, Department of Adult Education, 1972.

Aker, G. F., and Schroeder, W. L. (Eds.). *National Institute on Resource Development and Utilization in Adult Basic Education. Final Report.* Tallahassee: Florida State University, 1970.

Alexander, F., D., and Harshaw, J. *In-Service Training of Agricultural Agents in New York State:* Extension Study Number 6. Ithaca, N.Y.: Colleges of Agriculture and Home Economics at Cornell University, 1964.

Allison, G. T. *Essence of Decision.* Boston: Little, Brown, 1971.

Anderson, D., and Niemi, J. A. *Adult Education and the Disadvantaged Adult.* Syracuse, N.Y.: ERIC Clearinghouse on Adult Education, 1969.

Apps, J. W. "Tomorrow's Adult Education—Some Thoughts and Questions." *Adult Education,* 1972, *22* (3), 218-226.

Apps, J. W. *Toward a Working Philosophy of Education* (Occasional Paper No. 36). Syracuse, N.Y.: Syracuse University Publications in Continuing Education, 1973.

Argyris, C., and Schön, D. A. *Theory in Practice: Increasing Professional Effectiveness.* San Francisco: Jossey-Bass, 1976.

Baldridge, J. V., and Deal, T. E. *Managing Change in Education Organizations.* Berkeley, Calif.: McCutchan Publishing Corporation, 1975.

Beach, D. S. *Personnel: The Management of People at Work.* (3rd ed.) New York: Macmillan, 1975.

Beckerman, M. M. "Educational Change Agent: A New University Extension Professional Role." *Adult Leadership,* 1972, *21* (2), 39-40.

Beckhard, R. *Organization Development: Strategies and Models.* Reading, Mass.: Addison-Wesley, 1969.

Beder, H. W. "An Environmental Interaction Model for Agency Development in Adult Education." *Adult Education,* 1978, *28* (3), 176-190.

Bender, L. W. *Federal Regulations and Higher Education.* Higher Education Research Report No. 1. Washington, D.C.: American Association for Higher Education, 1977.

Bennis, W. G. *Organization Development: Its Nature, Origins, and Prospects.* Reading, Mass.: Addison-Wesley, 1969.

Bennis, W. G., Benne, K. D., Chin, R., and Corey, K. E. *The Planning of Change.* New York: Holt, Rinehart, and Winston, 1976.

Bergevin, P., Morris, D., and Smith, R. *Adult Education Procedures.* Greenwich, Conn.: Seabury Press, 1963.

Biddle, B. J., and Thomas, E. J. (Eds.). *Role Theory: Concepts and Research.* New York: Wiley, 1966.

Biddle, W., and Biddle, L. *The Community Development Process.* New York: Holt, Rinehart, and Winston, 1965.

Blake, R. R., and Mouton, J. S. *The Managerial Grid.* Houston, Texas: Gulf Publishing Company, 1964.

Blake, R. R., and Mouton, J. S. *Critique.* Rustin, Texas: Scientific Methods, 1976.

Blakely, R. J. "Is Adult Education Developing as a Profession?" *Continuous Learning,* 1966, *5* (4).

Blakely, R. J., and Lappin, I. M. *Knowledge Is Power to Control Power.* Syracuse, N.Y.: Syracuse University Publications in Continuing Education (Notes and Essays on Education for Adults, No. 63), 1969.

Block, J. H. "The 'C' in CPE." *Educational Researcher,* 1978, *7* (5), 13-16.

Blockstein, W. L., and Lemberger, A. P. "A Graduate Program in Pharmaceutical Extension." *American Journal of Pharmaceutical Education,* 1966, *30* (3), 473-477.

Boaz, R. L. *Participation in Adult Education: Final Report 1975.* Washington, D.C.: Department of Health, Education, and Welfare, National Center for Education Statistics, U.S. Government Printing Office, 1978.

Bolles, R. N. *The Three Boxes of Life.* Berkeley, Calif.: Ten Speed Press, 1978.

Boshier, R. "Educational Participation and Dropout: A Theoretical Model." *Adult Education,* 1973, *23* (4), 225-282.

Boshier, R. "Motivational Orientations Re-Visited: Life-Space Motives and the Education Participation Scale." *Adult Education,* 1977, *27* (2), 89-115.

Boyd, R. D. "New Designs for Adult Education Doctoral Programs." *Adult Education,* 1969, *19* (3), 186-196.

Bradford, L. P., Gibb, J. R., and Benne, K. D. (Eds.). *T-Group Theory and Laboratory Method.* New York: Wiley, 1964.

Bradshaw, J. "The Concept of Social Need." *Ekistics,* 1974, *220,* 184-187.

Brammer, L. M. *The Helping Relationship: Process and Skills.* Englewood Cliffs, N.J.: Prentice-Hall, 1973.
Brooke, W. M. "Profile, The Ontario Adult Basic Education Teacher." *Continuous Learning,* 1969, *8* (3), 103-111.
Broschart, J. R. *Lifelong Learning in the Nation's Third Century.* Washington, D.C.: United States Office of Education, Department of Health, Education, and Welfare (Publication Number OE 76-09102), U.S. Government Printing Office, 1977.
Broudy, H. S. "The Life Uses of Schooling as a Field for Research." In L. G. Thomas (Ed.), *Philosophical Redirection of Educational Research,* Seventy-first Yearbook of the National Society for the Study of Education, Part I. Chicago: University of Chicago Press, 1972.
Brown, E. B., and Dutton, D. *The Summer of '72: An Assessment of the Adult Basic Education Institutes in Tennessee, 1972.* Memphis: Memphis State University, 1972.
Brunner, E. DeS., and others. *An Overview of Adult Education Research.* Chicago: Adult Education Association of the U.S.A., 1959.
Bunch, D. K. "An Analysis of Courses, Course Content, and Subject Matter Areas Most Appropriate for Use in Development of a Master's Degree in Extension Education for Youth Workers." Unpublished master's thesis, Oklahoma State University, 1968.
Bunge, M. "The Role of Forecast in Planning." *Theory and Design,* 1973, *3,* 207-221.
Burns, T., and Stalker, G. M. *The Management of Innovation.* London: Tavistock Publications, 1961.
Butcher, D. G., and LeTarte, C. "Teacher Training for Adult Basic Education: Perceptions of a State Director of Adult Education." *Adult Leadership,* 1968, *17* (2), 81-82.
Campbell, D. D. *Adult Education as a Field of Study and Practice.* Vancouver, Canada: University of British Columbia, The Centre for Continuing Education, 1977.
Caplow, T. *How to Run Any Organization.* Hinsdale, Ill.: Dryden Press, 1967.
Carey, J. T. *Forms and Forces in University Adult Education.* Chicago: Center for the Study of Liberal Education for Adults, 1963.
Carter, L. F. "Knowledge Production and Utilization in Contemporary Organizations." In T. L. Eidell and L. M. Kitchel (Eds.), *Knowledge Production and Utilization in Educational Administration.* Eugene, Ore.: University of Oregon Press, 1968.
Chamberlain, M. N. "The Competencies of Adult Educators." *Adult Education,* 1961, *11* (2), 78-82.
Christoffel, P. H. "Future Federal Funding of Lifelong Learning." *Lifelong Learning: The Adult Years,* 1978, *1* (10), 17-24.
Clark, B. R. *Adult Education in Transition.* Berkeley: University of California Press, 1956.
Clark, H. E. "An Analysis of the Training Needs of Wisconsin County Extension Service Personnel." Unpublished doctoral dissertation, University of Wisconsin, 1960.

Cohen, M. D., and March, J. G. *Leadership and Ambiguity.* New York: McGraw-Hill, 1974.
Cook, B. D. "Comparative Analysis of the Training Needs for County Agents in Texas." Unpublished doctoral dissertation, University of Wisconsin, 1957.
Copeland, H. G. "The Specialization Issue in Adult Education Graduate Programs." *Andragogic,* 1973, *19* (3-4).
Craig, R. L. (Ed.). *Training and Development Handbook.* (2nd ed.) New York: McGraw-Hill, 1976.
Craven, R. M. "Factors Associated with Program Leadership of the State Leader of Home Economics Extension." Unpublished doctoral dissertation, University of Wisconsin, 1964.
Croft, F. A. "Competencies in Adult Education of Selected Episcopal Priests, with Implications for the Seminary Curriculum." Unpublished doctoral dissertation, Indiana University, 1964.
Cross, K. P., Valley, J. R., and others. *Planning Non-Traditional Programs.* San Francisco: Jossey-Bass, 1974.
Daigneault, G. H. *Decision Making in the University Evening College.* Chicago: Center for the Study of Liberal Education for Adults, 1963.
Darkenwald, G. G. "Innovation in Adult Education: An Organizational Analysis." *Adult Education,* 1977, *27* (3), 156-172.
Davies, I. K. *Competency-Based Learning: Technology, Management, and Design.* New York: McGraw-Hill, 1973.
Davis, G. A. *Psychology of Problem Solving: Theory and Practice.* New York: Basic Books, 1973.
Deppe, D. A. "The Adult Educator: Marginal Man and Boundary Definer." *Adult Leadership,* 1969, *18* (4), 119-120, 129, 130.
Dewey, J. *The Sources of a Science of Education.* New York: Liveright, 1929.
Dorland, J. R. "The Impact of Legislation on Adult Education." In N. C. Shaw (Ed.), *Administration of Continuing Education.* Washington: National Association for Public School Adult Education, 1969.
Douglah, M. A., and Moss, G. M. "Adult Education as a Field of Study and Its Implications for the Preparation of Adult Educators." *Adult Education,* 1969, *19* (2), 127-134.
Drucker, P. F. *The Effective Executive.* New York: Harper & Row, 1966.
Dutton, D., and others. *ABE Staff Development in Middle Tennessee.* Memphis: Memphis State University, 1972.
Eisner, E. W. "Educational Objectives: Help or Hindrance?" *School Review,* 1967, *75,* 250-266.
Eisner, E. W. "Instructional and Expressive Objectives: Their Formulation and Use in Curriculum." In *AERA Monograph Series on Curriculum Evaluation 3.* Chicago: Rand McNally, 1969.
ERIC/AE (Clearinghouse on Adult Education). *Personnel Development in Adult Education,* (Current Information Services, No. 31). Washington, D.C.: Adult Education Association, 1970.
Essert, P. L. "A Proposed New Program in Adult Education." *Adult Education,* 1960, *10* (3), 131-140.

Evans, R. I. *Resistance to Innovation in Higher Education.* San Francisco: Jossey-Bass, 1970.

Farmer, J. A., Jr. "Professionalization in Higher Adult Education Administration." *Adult Education,* 1970, *21* (1), 29-39.

Farmer, J. A., Jr., and Knox, A. B. *Alternative Patterns for Strengthening Community Service Programs in Institutions of Higher Education.* Urbana, Ill.: University of Illinois, 1977.

Farmer, M. L. *Counseling Services for Adults in Higher Education.* Metuchen, N.J.: Scarecrow Press, 1971.

Faure, E., and others. *Learning to Be.* Paris: UNESCO, 1972.

Flippo, E. B. *Principles of Personnel Management.* (4th ed.) New York: McGraw-Hill, 1976.

Foundation Directory. New York: Russell Sage Foundation, 1960 (Supplement No. 6, 1977).

Fox, D. J. *The Research Process in Education.* New York: Holt, Rinehart, and Winston, 1969.

Freire, P. "The Adult Literacy Process and Cultural Action for Freedom." *Harvard Educational Review,* 1970, *40* (2), 205-225.

Fuller, J. W. "An In-Service Program for Adult Education Faculty." *Adult Leadership,* 1971, *20,* 205-206.

Gardner, J. W. *Self-Renewal: The Individual and the Innovative Society.* New York: Harper & Row, 1964.

Gassie, E. W. "Factors Associated with Job Performance of Assistant and Associate County Agents Doing 4-H Club Work, Louisiana." Unpublished doctoral dissertation, Louisiana State University, 1965.

Gladieux, L. E., and Wolanin, T. R. "Federal Politics." In D. W. Breneman and C. E. Finn (Eds.), *Public Policy and Private Higher Education.* Washington, D.C.: Brookings Institution, 1978.

Glaser, R. "Components of a Psychology of Instruction: Towards a Science of Design." *Review of Educational Research,* 1976, *46,* 1-24.

Goldstein, A. P., and Sorcher, M. *Changing Supervisor Behavior.* New York: Pergamon Press, 1973.

Gossage, L. C. "The Qualifications and Educational Needs of Industrial Training Directors." Unpublished doctoral dissertation, University of California at Los Angeles, 1967.

Gould, R. *Transformations.* New York: Simon and Schuster, 1978.

Grabowski, S. M. *Training Teachers of Adults: Models and Summative Programs.* Syracuse, N.Y.: Syracuse University, 1976.

Grattan, C. H. *In Quest of Knowledge.* New York: Association Press, 1955.

Grattan, C. H. *In Quest of Knowledge: A Historical Perspective on Adult Education.* (reprint) New York: Arno Press and The *New York Times,* 1971.

Griffith, W. S. *Administrative Competencies Essential to the Optimum Utilization of Resource Development and Utilization in Adult Basic Education.* Chicago: University of Chicago, 1970.

Griffith, W. S. "Adult Educators and Politics." *Adult Education,* 1976, *26* (4), 270-297.

Griffith, W. S., and Cervero, R. M. "The Adult Performance Level Program: A Serious and Deliberate Examination." *Adult Education,* 1977, *27* (4), 209-224.

Griffith, W. S., and Cloutier, G. H. *A Directory and Analysis of Degree Programs for Preparing Professional Adult Educators in the United States.* Chicago: University of Chicago, 1972.

Griffith, W. S., and Cloutier, G. H. *College and University Degree Programs for the Preparation of Professional Adult Educators, 1970-71.* DHEW Publication Number (OE) 74-11423, U.S. Office of Education, Department of Health, Education, and Welfare, 1974.

Griffith, W. S., and Hayes, A. P. (Eds.). *Adult Basic Education: The State of the Art.* Chicago: University of Chicago, 1970.

Gross, R., and Osterman, P. (Eds.). *The New Professionals.* New York: Simon and Schuster, 1972.

Grotelueschen, A. D., Gooler, D. D., and Knox, A. B. *Evaluation in Adult Basic Education: How and Why.* Danville, Ill.: Interstate, 1976.

Hackman, J. R., and Oldham, G. R. "Development of the Job Diagnostic Survey." *Journal of Applied Psychology,* 1975, *60,* 159-170.

Hackman, J. R., and others. "A New Strategy for Job Enrichment." *California Management Review,* 1975, *17* (4), 57-71.

Hall, D. T. *Careers in Organizations.* Pacific Palisades, Calif.: Goodyear, 1976.

Hall, G. E., and Jones, H. L. *Competency-Based Education: A Process for the Improvement of Education.* Englewood Cliffs, N.J.: Prentice-Hall, 1976.

Hansen, G. L., Klink, A. L., and Kramer, R. E. *Assessment and Programming for Personnel Development in Adult Education—State of Iowa.* Iowa: University of Northern Iowa, 1973.

Harris, B. M., and Bessent, W. *In-Service Education.* Englewood Cliffs: Prentice-Hall, 1969.

Havelock, R. G. *Planning for Innovation.* Ann Arbor: Center for Research on the Utilization of Scientific Knowledge, University of Michigan, 1969.

Havelock, R. G., and Havelock, M. *Training for Change Agents.* Ann Arbor: Center for Research on the Utilization of Scientific Knowledge, University of Michigan, 1972.

Havighurst, R. J., and Orr, B. *Adult Education and Adult Needs.* Chicago: Center for the Study of Liberal Education for Adults, 1956.

Heffernan, J. M., Macy, F. V., and Vickers, D. F. *Educational Brokering: A New Service for Adult Learners.* Syracuse, N.Y.: National Center for Educational Brokering, 1976.

Hentschke, G. C. *Management Operations in Education.* Berkeley, Calif.: McCutchan Publishing Corporation, 1975.

Heroux, G. A. *Continuing Professional Education.* Springfield, Ill.: Illinois Institute for Continuing Legal Education, 1975.

Hoppe, W. W. (Ed.). *Policies and Practices in Evening Colleges.* Metuchen, N.J.: Scarecrow Press, 1969.

Houle, C. O. "Professional Education for Educators of Adults." *Adult Education,* 1956, *6* (3), 137-139.

Houle, C. O. *Proceedings of the Fifth Leadership Conference for University Adult Educators.* Chicago: Center for the Study of Liberal Education for Adults, 1957.

Houle, C. O. *The Effective Board.* New York: Association Press, 1960.

Houle, C. O. *The Inquiring Mind.* Madison: University of Wisconsin Press, 1961.

Houle, C. O. "The Emergence of Graduate Study in Adult Education." In G. Jensen, A. A. Liveright, and W. Hallenbeck (Eds.), *Adult Education: Outlines of an Emerging Field of University Study.* Washington, D.C.: Adult Education Association of the U.S.A., 1964.

Houle, C. O. "Federal Policies Concerning Adult Education." *The School Review,* 1968, *76,* 166-189.

Houle, C. O. "The Educators of Adults." In M. Smith, G. F. Aker, and J. R. Kidd (Eds.), *Handbook of Adult Education.* New York: Macmillan, 1970.

Houle, C. O. *The Design of Education.* San Francisco: Jossey-Bass, 1972.

Houle, C. O. "Who Stays and Why?" *Adult Education,* 1974, *14* (4), 225-233.

House, F. *The Politics of Educational Innovation.* Berkeley, Calif.: McCutchan, 1974.

Howe, M. J. A. (Ed.). *Adult Learning: Psychological Research and Applications.* London: Wiley, 1977.

Hoyt, H. P. "The Recipients of the Doctorate in Adult Education—Their Morale and Their Perception of Themselves as Opinion Leaders." Unpublished doctoral dissertation, University of Wyoming, 1969.

Ingham, R. J. *Design and Operation of Educative Systems.* Tallahassee: Florida State University, 1972 (mimeographed).

Ingham, R. J., and Hanks, G. *An Ideal Curriculum for Professional Education: Applications to Adult Education.* Tallahassee: Florida State University, Department of Adult Education, April 1978 (mimeographed).

Ingham, R. J., and Qazilbash, H. *A Survey of Graduate Programs in Adult Education in the United States and Canada.* Tallahassee: Florida State University, Department of Adult Education, 1968 (mimeographed).

Ingham, R. J., and Robbins, J. N. *Survey of Graduate Programs in the United States and Canada.* Tallahassee: Florida State University, Program for the Design and Management of Post-Secondary Education, 1976-77. A Survey Questionnaire, 1977 (mimeographed).

Jantsch, E. *Design for Evolution.* New York: George Braziller, 1975.

Jensen, G. S. *A Report on the 1968 Adult Basic Education Institute for Administrators in Region VII.* Laramie: University of Wyoming, 1969.

Jensen, G. S., Liveright, A. A., and Hallenbeck, W. (Eds.). *Adult Education: Outlines of an Emerging Field of University Study.* Washington, D.C.: Adult Education Association of the U.S.A., 1964.

Johnson, E. I. *Metroplex Assembly: An Experiment on Community Education.* Reports, No. 213. Boston: Center for the Study of Liberal Education for Adults, 1965.

Johnstone, J. W. C., and Rivera, R. *Volunteers for Learning.* Chicago: Aldine, 1965.

Jones, C. I. "Factors Related to the Effectiveness of Teachers of Short-Term Adult Vocational Courses." Unpublished doctoral dissertation, Florida State University, 1967.

Joyce, B., and Weil, M. *Models of Teaching*. Englewood Cliffs, N.J.: Prentice-Hall, 1972.

Katz, D., and Kahn, R. L. *The Social Psychology of Organizations*. New York: Wiley, 1966.

Kemmis, S., and Stake, R. E. "Operational vs. Judgmental Assessment of Teacher Competence." *Educational Leadership*, 1974, *31* (4), 322-325.

Kent, W. P. *A Longitudinal Evaluation of the Adult Basic Education Program*. Falls Church, Virg.: System Development Corporation, 1973.

Kerlinger, F. N. *Foundations of Behavioral Research*. (2nd ed.) New York: Holt, Rinehart, and Winston, 1973.

Kerr, D. H. *Educational Policy: Analysis, Structure, and Justification*. New York: David McKay, 1976.

Kidd, J. R. *Financing Continuing Education*. New York: Scarecrow Press, 1962.

Kincaid, H. V., and Rink, D. L. *Preliminary Three-Year Plan for Adult Basic Education Staff Development*. Menlo Park, Calif.: Stanford Research Institute, 1972.

Klevins, C. (Ed.). *Materials and Methods in Adult Education*. New York: Klevens Publications, Inc., 1972.

Knowles, M. S. "A General Theory of the Doctorate in Education." *Adult Education*, 1962, *12*, 136-141.

Knowles, M. S. *Higher Adult Education in the United States*. Washington, D.C.: American Council on Education, 1969.

Knowles, M. S. *The Modern Practice of Adult Education*. New York: Association Press, 1970.

Knowles, M. S. *Self Directed Learning*. New York: Association Press, 1975.

Knowles, M. S. *A History of the Adult Education Movement in the United States*. (rev. ed.) Huntington, N.Y.: Krieger, 1977.

Knox, A. B. "Continuous Program Evaluation." In N. Shaw (Ed.), *Administration of Continuing Education*. Washington, D.C.: National Association for Public School Adult Education, 1969.

Knox, A. B. *In-Service Education in Adult Basic Education*. Tallahassee: Florida State University, 1971.

Knox, A. B. *Development of Adult Education Graduate Programs*. Washington, D.C.: Commission of the Professors of Adult Education, Adult Education Association of the U.S.A., 1973.

Knox, A. B. "Life-Long Self-Directed Education." In R. J. Blakely (Ed.), *Fostering the Growing Need to Learn*. Rockville, Md.: Division of Regional Medical Programs, Bureau of Health Resources Development, 1974.

Knox, A. B. "New Realities in the Administration of Continuing Higher Education." *The NUEA Spectator*, 1975, *39* (22), 6-9.

Knox, A. B. *Helping Adults to Learn*. (Concept Paper #4) Washington, D.C.: The Continuing Library Education Network and Exchange, 1976.

Knox, A. B. *Adult Development and Learning: A Handbook on Individual Growth and Competence in the Adult Years for Education and the Helping Professions.* San Francisco: Jossey-Bass, 1977a.

Knox, A. B. *Current Research Needs Related to Systematic Learning by Adults.* (Occasional Paper No. 4) Urbana: University of Illinois, 1977b.

Knox, A. B. (Ed.). *Adult Education Program Development and Administration.* San Francisco: Jossey-Bass, forthcoming.

Knox, A. B., and Farmer, H. S. "Overview of Counseling and Information Services for Adult Learners." *International Review of Education,* 1977, *23* (4), 387-414.

Knox, A. B., and others. *An Evaluation Guide for Adult Basic Education Programs.* Washington: U.S. Government Printing Office, 1974.

Kogan, M., and Packwood, T. *Advisory Councils and Committees in Education.* Boston: Routledge & K. Paul, 1974.

Kotler, P. *Marketing for Non-Profit Organizations.* Englewood Cliffs, N.J.: Prentice-Hall, 1974.

Kozoll, C. E. *Staff Development in Organizations.* Reading, Mass.: Addison-Wesley, 1974.

Kreitlow, B. W. "Professional Education for Educators of Adults." *Adult Education,* 1956, *6* (3), 147-148.

Kreitlow, B. W. *Educating the Adult Educator: Part I, Concepts for the Curriculum.* Madison: University of Wisconsin-Madison, March 1965. (Also published as Bulletin 573, Washington, D.C.: Department of Agriculture, 1965.)

Lauffer, A. *The Practice of Continuing Education in the Human Services.* New York: McGraw-Hill, 1977.

Lawrence, P. R., and Lorsch, J. W. *Developing Organizations: Diagnosis and Action.* Reading, Mass.: Addison-Wesley, 1969.

Leagans, P., Copeland, H., and Kaiser, G. *Selected Concepts from Educational Psychology and Adult Education for Extension and Continuing Educators.* (Notes and Essays on Education for Adults, No. 71) Syracuse, N.Y.: Syracuse University, Publications in Continuing Education, 1971.

Levine, H. A. "Collective Bargaining and Educational Opportunity." *Training and Development Journal,* 1977, *31* (6), 50-56.

Levinson, D. J., and others. *The Seasons of a Man's Life.* New York: Knopf, 1978.

Lindquist, J. *Strategies for Change.* Berkeley, Calif.: Pacific Soundings Press, 1978.

Lippitt, G., and Nadler, L. "Emerging Roles of the Training Director: Is Training Sufficiently Creative and Innovative to Serve Its Full Purpose?" *Training and Development Journal,* 1967, *21* (8), 2-10.

London, J., Wenkert, R., and Hagstrom, W. O. *Adult Education and Social Class.* (Cooperative Research Project No. 1017, USOE) Berkeley, Calif.: University of California, Survey Research Center, 1963.

Long, H. B., and Agyekum, S. K. "Adult Education 1964-1973: Reflections of a Changing Discipline." *Adult Education,* 1974, *24* (2), 99-120.

Lowe, J. *The Education of Adults: A World Perspective.* Paris: UNESCO Press, 1975.

McKinley, J. "Perspectives on Diagnostics in Adult Education." *Viewpoints, Bulletin of the School of Education, Indiana University,* 1973, *49* (5), 69-83.

Madry, A. C. "The Functions and Training Needs of Adult Education Directors in Public School." Unpublished doctoral dissertation, Ohio State University, 1963.

Mager, R. F. *Preparing Instructional Objectives.* San Francisco: Fearon Publishers, 1962.

Mager, R., and Pipe, P. *Analyzing Performance Problems.* Belmont, Calif.: Fearon Publishers, 1972.

Mann, D. *Policy Decision-Making in Education.* New York: Teachers College Press, Columbia University, 1975.

Marshall, L. E. (Ed.). *Adult Basic Education Administrators' Institute, Region II.* Upper Montclair, N.J.: Montclair State College, 1968.

Mathieson, D. E. *Correspondence Study: A Summary Review of the Research and Development Literature.* Syracuse, N.Y.: National Home Study Council and ERIC Clearinghouse on Adult Education, 1971.

Mayhew, L. B., and Ford, P. J. *Reform in Graduate and Professional Education.* San Francisco: Jossey-Bass, 1974.

Messerschmidt, D. H. "A Study of Part-Time Instructors in Vocational-Technical Education among Community Colleges in Michigan." Unpublished doctoral dissertation, Michigan State University, 1967.

Metcalfe, W. W. "Concepts of Education Held by Informal Adult Educators." Unpublished doctoral dissertation, University of Chicago, 1965.

Mezirow, J. "Perspective Transformation." *Adult Education,* 1978, *28* (2), 100-110.

Mezirow, J., Darkenwald, G., and Knox, A. B. *Last Gamble on Education.* Washington, D.C.: Adult Education Association of the U.S.A., 1975.

Miles, M. B. "Changes During and Following Laboratory Training: A Clinical-Experimental Study." *The Journal of Applied Behavioral Science,* 1965, *1* (3), 215-242.

Miller, D. B. *Personal Vitality.* Reading, Mass.: Addison-Wesley, 1977.

Miller, G. A., Galanter, E., and Pribram, K. H. *Plans and the Structure of Behavior.* New York: Holt, Rinehart, and Winston, 1960.

Miller, H. L. *Teaching and Learning in Adult Education.* New York: Macmillan, 1964.

Miller, H. L. *Participation of Adults in Education: A Force Field Analysis.* Syracuse, N.Y.: Center for the Study of Liberal Education of Adults, Syracuse University, 1967.

Mintzberg, H. *The Nature of Managerial Work.* New York: Harper & Row, 1973.

Mocker, D. W. *A Report on the Identification, Classification, and Ranking of Competencies Appropriate for Adult Basic Education Teachers.* Kansas City: University of Missouri-Kansas City, 1974.

Monette, M. L. "The Concept of Educational Need." *Adult Education,* 1977, *27* (2), 116-127.

Moore, D. J. "An Analysis of the Relationship of Certain Employee Characteristics to Tenure and Performance of Selected Virginia Extension Agents—Agriculture." Unpublished master's thesis, University of Maryland, 1967.

Murray, N. J. M. "Competency-Based Learning Packages— A Case Study." *Training and Development Journal,* 1976, *30* (9), 3–7.

Newell, A., and Simon, H. A. *Human Problem Solving.* Englewood Cliffs, N.J.: Prentice-Hall, 1972.

Niemi, J. A., Grabowski, S. M., and Kuusisto, E. A. (Eds.). *Research and Investigation in Adult Education.* (1976 Annual Register) DeKalb: Northern Illinois University, ERIC Clearinghouse in Career Education, 1976.

Niemi, J. A., and Jessen, D. C. *Directory of Resources in Adult Education.* Washington, D.C.: Adult Education Association and ERIC Clearinghouse in Career Education at Northern Illinois University, 1976.

Noel, J. L., and Parsons, J. "Doctoral Graduates Evaluate the Relevance of Departmental Learning Objectives to Their Professional Responsibilities." *Adult Education,* 1973, *24* (1), 43–54.

Okes, I. *Participation in Adult Education, Final Report 1972.* Washington, D.C.: Department of Health, Education, and Welfare, National Center for Education Statistics, U.S. Government Printing Office, 1976.

Osborn, A. F. *Applied Imagination.* New York: Scribner, 1953.

Palmer, R., and others. *Leadership Skills in Adult Basic Education: A Resource Document and Workshop Report.* Tallahassee: Florida State University, Department of Adult Education, 1969.

Parker, B., and Paisley, J. *Patterns of Adult Information Seeking.* Stanford: Stanford University (Final Report on United States Office of Education Project No. 2583), 1966.

Peabody, F. J. "An Analysis of Critical Incidents for Recently Employed Michigan Cooperative Extension Agents with Implication for Training." Unpublished doctoral dissertation, Michigan State University, 1968.

Penfield, K. R. "Public Service vs. Academic Values: University Extension in Conflict." *Adult Education,* 1975, *25* (2), 107–124.

Pennington, F., and Green, J. "Comparative Analysis of Program Development Processes in Six Professions." *Adult Education,* 1976, *27* (1), 13–23.

Pepper, S. *The Sources of Value.* Berkeley, Calif.: University of California Press, 1958.

Perrone, P., and Davis, S. A. *Adult Counseling Project.* Madison: University of Wisconsin, Center for Studies in Vocational and Technical Education, 1976.

Phi Delta Kappan. Special issue on minimum competency testing. 1978, *59* (1).

Pitchell, R. J. "Financing Part-Time Students." In D. W. Vermilye (Ed.), *Lifelong Learners—A New Clientele for Higher Education: Current Issues in Higher Education 1974.* San Francisco: Jossey-Bass, 1974.

Porter, L. *Faculty Perceptions of Continuing Education at Syracuse University.* (Occasional Paper Number 20) Syracuse, N.Y.: Syracuse University Publications in Continuing Education, 1970.

Price, R. K. "An Analysis of Educational Needs of Arkansas Extension Agents." Unpublished doctoral dissertation, University of Wisconsin, 1960.

Richman, B. M., and Farmer, R. N. *Leadership, Goals and Power in Higher Education: A Contingency and Open-Systems Approach to Effective Management.* San Francisco: Jossey-Bass, 1974.

Riggs, J. A. "The Relationship between the Education, Background Experiences, and Personal Traits of Counselors of Adults, and the Ability of the Counselors to Establish Rapport When Counseling Adult Clients." Unpublished doctoral dissertation, University of Illinois, 1978.

Robinson, C. O. "Criteria for the Education of Adult Educators." *Adult Education,* 1962, *12* (4), 243-245.

Rogers, J. *Adults Learning.* Baltimore: Penguin Education, 1971.

Rose, H. (Comp.). *Appalachian Adult Basic Education Teacher-Training Workshop.* Morehead, Kent.: Appalachian Adult Basic Education Demonstration Center, 1969.

Rossman, M. H., and Bunning, R. L. "Knowledge and Skills for the Adult Educator: A Delphi Study." *Adult Education,* 1978, *28* (3), 139-155.

Ruesch, J. *Knowledge in Action.* New York: Jason Aronson, 1975.

Sager, G. A. "Staffing the Evening College, a Study of Twelve Institutions in the Middle Atlantic Region." Unpublished doctoral dissertation, University of Wisconsin, 1963.

Sagoff, S. E. *Adults in Transition.* Winchester, Mass.: The New England Board of Higher Education, 1965.

Scates, A. Y. "Professional Preparation for Educators of Adults: A Survey of the Status and Content of Graduate Programs in Adult Education." Unpublished doctoral dissertation, George Washington University, 1963.

Schein, E. H. *Career Dynamics: Matching Individual and Organizational Needs.* Reading, Mass.: Addison-Wesley, 1978.

Schneider, B. *Staffing Organizations.* Pacific Palisades, Calif.: Goodyear, 1976.

Seaman, D. F., and others. *Behavioral Skills for Adult Basic Education: A Resource Document and Institute Report.* State College: Mississippi State University, 1969.

Sergiovanni, T. J. *Emerging Patterns of Supervision: Human Perspectives.* New York: McGraw-Hill, 1971.

Sharma, J. C. "A Time-Use Analysis of the Agricultural Agents in New York State." Unpublished doctoral dissertation, Cornell University, 1963.

Shaw, N. C. (Ed.). *Administration of Continuing Education.* Washington, D.C.: National Association for Public School Adult Education, 1969.

Simon, H. A. *The Sciences of the Artificial.* Cambridge: Massachusetts Institute of Technology Press, 1969.

Smith, R. M. *Learning How to Learn in Adult Education.* (Information Series No. 10) DeKalb, Ill.: ERIC Clearinghouse in Career Education, 1976.

Smith, R. M., Aker, G. F., and Kidd, J. R. (Eds.). *Handbook of Adult Education.* New York: Macmillan, 1970.

Smith, R. M., and Haverkamp, K. K. "Towards a Theory of Learning How to Learn." *Adult Education,* 1977, *28* (1), 3-21.

Solomon, D., Bezdek, W. E., and Rosenberg, L. *Teaching Styles and Learning.* Chicago: Center for the Study of Liberal Education for Adults, 1963.

Southern Regional Education Board. *Readings in Staff Development.* Atlanta, Geo.: Southern Regional Education Board, 1971.

Spady, W. G. "Competency Based Education: A Bandwagon in Search of a Definition." *Educational Researcher,* 1977, *6* (1), 9-14.

Spady, W. G., and Mitchell, D. E. "Competency Based Education: Organizational Issues and Implications." *Educational Researcher,* 1977, *6* (2), 9-15.

Spear, G. E. (Ed.). *Adult Education Staff Development: Selected Issues, Alternatives, and Implications.* Kansas City: University of Missouri-Kansas City, Center for Resource Development in Adult Education, 1976.

Stake, R. E. "The Countenance of Educational Evaluation." *Teachers College Record,* 1967, *68,* 523-540.

Steele, S. M. *Contemporary Approaches to Program Evaluation and Their Implications for Evaluating Programs for Disadvantaged Adults.* Syracuse, N.Y.: ERIC Clearinghouse on Adult Education, 1973.

Steinberg, S. S., and Fishman, J. R. *New Careers: The Teacher Aide. A Manual for Trainers.* Washington, D.C.: University Research Corp., nd. (Also available from New Careers Institute, University Research Corp., 1424 16th St., N.W., Washington, D.C. 20036.)

Stenzel, A. K. "A Study of Girl Scout Leadership Training, Non-Professional Leaders of Adults as Continuous Learners." Unpublished doctoral dissertation, University of California at Berkeley, 1963.

Stenzel, A. K., and Feeney, H. M. *Learning by the Case Method.* New York: Seabury Press, 1970.

Stufflebeam, D. L. *Meta-Evaluation.* Kalamazoo: Western Michigan University, Evaluation Center, 1974.

Swanson, H. B., and Carter, G. L. "What Motivates Educators to Improve?" *Minnesota Science,* 1967, *23,* 10-12.

Thomas, A. "The Making of a Professional." In J. R. Kidd (Ed.), *Learning and Society.* Toronto: Canadian Association for Adult Education, 1963, 336-344.

Torshen, K. P. *The Mastery Approach to Competency-Based Education.* New York: Academic Press, 1977.

Tough, A. *Learning Without a Teacher.* (Educational Research Series No. 3) Toronto: Ontario Institute for Studies in Education, 1967.

Tough, A. "Adult Education as a Field of Study in Canada." *Continuous Learning,* 1968a, *7,* 4-14.

Tough, A. *Why Adults Learn: A Study of the Major Reasons for Beginning and Continuing a Learning Project.* Toronto: Ontario Institute for Studies in Education, 1968b.

Tough, A. *The Adult's Learning Projects.* (Research in Education Series No. 1) Toronto: Ontario Institute for Studies in Education, 1971.

Tough, A. "Major Learning Efforts: Recent Research and Future Directions." *Adult Education,* 1978, *28* (4), 250-263.

Travers, R. M. W. (Ed.). *Second Handbook of Research on Teaching.* Chicago: Rand McNally, 1973.

Trivett, D. A. *Competency Programs in Higher Education.* Washington, D.C.: American Association for Higher Education, 1975.

Tyler, R. W. *Basic Principles of Curriculum and Instruction.* (Syllabus for Education 305) Chicago: University of Chicago Press, 1950.

Ulmer, C. *Teaching the Disadvantaged Adult.* Washington, D.C.: National Association for Public School Adult Education, 1969.

Ussery, M. A. "An Analysis of the Educational Needs of County Extension Agents in Tennessee." Unpublished doctoral dissertation, University of Wisconsin, 1964.

Vaillant, G. *Adaptation to Life.* Boston: Little, Brown, 1977.

Van Maanen, J. (Ed.). *Organizational Careers.* New York: Wiley, 1977.

Veri, C. C. "The Design of a Doctoral Degree Program in Adult Education Based on the Professed Needs of the Professional Practitioners." Unpublished doctoral dissertation, University of Nebraska, 1968.

Veri, C. C. *A Proposed Process for Determining Professional Behavior Needed by Adult Education Administrators.* St. Louis: University of Missouri, nd.

Verner, C., Dickinson, G., Leirman, W., and Niskala, H. *The Preparation of Adult Educators.* Washington, D.C.: ERIC Clearinghouse on Adult Education and Adult Education Association of the U.S.A., 1970.

Vontress, C. E., and Thomas, H. A. "Counseling Adults." *Adult Leadership,* 1968, *17* (6), 279-281.

Warren, V. B. *A Guide for Teacher Trainers in Adult Basic Education.* Washington, D.C.: National Association for Public School Adult Education, 1966.

Whipple, J. B. *Especially for Adults.* Chicago: Center for the Study of Liberal Education for Adults, 1957.

White, R. W. *Lives in Progress.* New York: Holt, Rinehart, and Winston, 1961.

White, R. W. (Ed.). *Study of Lives.* New York: Atherton Press, 1963.

White, R. W. *The Enterprise of Living.* New York: Holt, Rinehart, and Winston, 1972.

White, T. "Some Common Interests of Adult Education Leaders." *Adult Education,* 1956, *6* (3), 155-161.

Wientge, K. M. "Adult Teacher Self Improvement Through Evaluation by Students." *Adult Education,* 1968, *18* (2), 94-100.

Williams, F. N. "The Neglected Teachers: The Part Time Faculty." *Adult Leadership,* 1972, *21* (3), 83, 84.

Wirt, F. M. *The Polity of the School: New Research in Educational Politics.* Lexington, Mass.: Lexington Books, D. C. Heath and Co., 1975.

Woeste, J. T. "An Analysis of the Association of Selected Factors to Job Performance of Cooperative Extension Area-Specialists." Unpublished doctoral dissertation, University of Wisconsin, 1967.

Worthen, B. R., and Sanders, J. R. *Educational Evaluation: Theory and Practice.* Belmont, Calif.: Wadsworth, 1973.

Ziegler, W. L. (Ed.). *Essays on the Future of Continuing Education.* Notes and Essays on Education for Adults, Number 66. Syracuse, N.Y.: Syracuse University Publications in Continuing Education, 1970.

Zinn, L. M. *Adult Basic Education Teacher Competency Inventory: Iowa, Final Report.* Kansas City: University of Missouri-Kansas City, Center for Resource Development in Adult Education, 1974.

index

A

Adelson, M., 5, 19, 79
Administration, as administrator proficiency, 23, 25-30, 68, 71-72
Administrators: areas of proficiency for, 25-36; future proficiency of, 38-40; need for proficiency by, 24-25; policy issues related to, 39-40; powerlessness of, 29, 39, 72; proficiency of, 2, 18-19, 23-41, 71-74. *See also* Practitioners
Adult basic education (ABE): counseling in, 27; funds for, 62; and resource persons, 7, 46, 47, 55, 68, 75
Adult Education Association, 7, 37
Adults: development of, 13-15, 47, 48, 54, 69-70, 74; financial assistance to, 28, 39, 40; as learners, 9, 13-17, 21, 68, 69-70
Agencies: increasing proficiency through, 37, 73; types and functioning of, 10, 21
Agency director, as administrator, 23
Agyekum, S. K., 3, 87
Aker, G. F., 3, 5, 7, 10, 31, 60, 68, 69, 71, 72, 79, 90
Alexander, F. D., 46, 79
Allison, G. T., 29, 79
Anderson, D., 26, 27, 79
Apps, J. W., 3, 30, 31, 69, 79
Argyris, C., 19, 70, 79

B

Baldridge, J. V., 30, 79
Beach, D. S., 28, 80
Beckerman, M. M., 30, 80
Beckhard, R., 28, 72, 80
Beder, H. W., 30, 80
Bender, L. W., 60, 80
Benne, K. D., 11, 34, 69, 70, 75, 80
Bennis, W. G., 11, 28, 69, 72, 80
Bergevin, P., 50, 80
Bessent, W., 28, 84
Bezdek, W. E., 34, 73, 90
Biddle, B. J., 29, 80
Biddle, L., 34, 75, 80
Biddle, W., 34, 75, 80
Blake, R. R., 7, 29, 71, 80
Blakely, R. J., 3, 11, 69, 80
Block, J. H., 6, 80
Blockstein, W. L., 45, 80
Boaz, R. L., 26, 71, 80
Bolles, R. N., 15, 80
Boshier, R., 26, 80
Boyd, R. D., 3, 80
Bradford, L. P., 34, 70, 75, 80
Bradshaw, J., 31, 80
Brammer, L. M., 81
Brooke, W. M., 45, 81
Broschart, J. R., 59, 62, 69, 81
Broudy, H. S., 6, 81
Brown, E. B., 45, 81
Brunner, E. DeS., 35, 81
Bunch, D., K., 3, 81
Bunge, M., 5, 81
Bunning, R. L., 3, 9, 90
Burns, T., 29, 81
Butcher, D. G., 45, 81

C

Campbell, D. D., 3, 5, 7, 9, 17, 68, 81
Caplow, T., 29, 71, 81
Carey, J. T., 69, 81
Carter, G. L., 6, 91
Carter, L. F., 5, 81
Cervero, R. M., 6, 84
Chamberlain, M. N., 3, 5, 7, 10, 81
Chin, R., 11, 69, 80
Christoffel, P. H., 62, 63, 81
Clark, B. R., 69, 81
Clark, H. E., 45, 81
Cloutier, G. H., 3, 84
Cohen, M. D., 19, 29, 30, 69, 72, 82
Commitment to lifelong learning, as personal quality, 18, 68, 70
Competence, concept of, 4
Competency-based education, 5-6, 7
Context: of resources, 32-33, 72; societal, and resource persons, 48-49, 75
Continuing education: future of, 67-77; overview of, 1-8; trends in, 2
Cooperative Extension Service (CES): funds for, 62; and policy makers, 61;

93

Cooperative Extension Service *(cont'd.)* program success in, 6, 35; and resource persons, 7, 43, 52, 55, 68, 75; training by, 7, 25
Cook, B. D., 46, 82
Copeland, H., 5, 31, 87
Copeland, H. G., 3, 5, 82
Corey, K. E., 11, 69, 80
Counselors. *See* Resource persons
Craig, R. L., 21, 75, 82
Craven, R. M., 24, 82
Creativity, as personal quality, 5, 19-20, 68, 70
Croft, F. A., 46, 82
Cross, K. P., 34, 82

D

Daigneault, G. H., 69, 82
Darkenwald, G. G., 21, 28, 30, 31, 69, 72, 82, 88
Davies, I. K., 6, 82
Davis, G. A., 20, 82
Davis, S. A., 26, 89
Deal, T. E., 30, 79
Deppe, D. A., 24, 82
Dewey, J., 5, 82
Dickinson, G., 3, 5, 7, 9, 68, 92
Direct action, increasing proficiency through, 38-39, 54-55
Dorland, J. R., 28, 82
Douglah, M. A., 7, 82
Drucker, P. F., 29, 71, 82
Dutton, D., 45, 81, 82

E

Educational institutions: administrators for, 23, 25; as parent organization, 2, 10, 11, 69; and policy makers, 61; resource persons in, 43-44, 52-53, 55-56; use of proficiency by, 20-21, 22; workshops of, 7
Eisner, E. W., 6, 82
Employer: administrators for, 23; as parent organization, 2, 10, 11, 21, 69; and policy makers, 61; program success to, 6, 35; and resource persons, 53, 55; workshops of, 7
ERIC/AE, 9, 82
Essert, P. L., 3, 82
Evaluation, of programs, 34-35, 39, 51-52, 55, 73, 75
Evans, R., I., 60, 83
Experience, increasing proficiency through, 10, 11, 14, 15, 17, 69, 70

F

Farmer, H. S., 19, 26, 27, 44, 74, 87
Farmer, J. A., Jr., 21, 24, 30, 39, 69, 72, 83
Farmer, M. L., 26, 74, 83
Farmer, R. N., 30, 90
Faure, E., 59, 83
Feeney, H. M., 34, 75, 91
Fishman, J. R., 45, 91
Flippo, E. B., 28, 71, 83
Ford, P. J., 60, 88
Foundations, philanthropic, 62, 76
Fox, D. J., 36, 83
Freire, P., 32, 83
Fuller, J. W., 83

G

Galanter, E., 5, 20, 88
Gardner, J. W., 19, 83
Gassie, E. W., 45, 83
Gibb, J. R., 34, 70, 75, 80
Gladieux, L. E., 60, 63, 83
Glaser, R., 5, 83
Goldstein, A. P., 28, 83
Gooler, D. D., 34, 73, 84
Gossage, L. C., 24, 83
Gould, R., 15, 83
Government agencies, and policy makers, 61-62, 76
Grabowski, S. M., 28, 35, 45, 83, 89
Graduate study, 7, 38, 74
Grant proposals, 12-13, 69
Grattan, C. H., 11, 12, 69, 83
Green, J., 31, 72, 89
Griffith, W. S., 3, 6, 24, 60, 62, 63, 65, 83-84
Gross, R., 5, 84
Grotelueschen, A. D., 34, 73, 84

H

Hackman, J. R., 21, 28, 61, 70, 84
Hagstrom, W. O., 26, 27, 71, 87
Hall, D. T., 28, 64
Hall, G. E., 6, 84
Hallenbeck, W., 10, 24, 25, 68, 85
Hanberry, G. C., 60, 79
Hanks, G., 17, 19, 85
Hansen, G. L., 9, 45, 47, 84

Harris, B. M., 28, 84
Harshaw, J., 46, 79
Havelock, M., 28, 84
Havelock, R. G., 28, 31, 72, 84
Haverkamp, K. K., 17, 90
Havighurst, R. J., 32, 84
Hayes, A. P., 24, 84
Heffernan, J. M., 27, 74, 84
Hentschke, G. C., 28, 71, 84
Heroux, G. A., 24, 84
Hoppe, W. W., 29, 84
Hospitals, as parent organization, 2
Houle, C. O., 3, 10, 26, 30, 33, 62, 68, 70, 72, 75, 76, 85
House, F., 30, 60, 85
Howe, M. J. A., 15, 70, 85
Hoyt, H. P., 3, 85

I

Ingham, R. J., 3, 7, 17, 19, 20, 85
Interpersonal effectiveness, as personal quality, 18-19, 68, 70

J

Jantsch, E., 5, 20, 85
Jensen, G. S., 10, 24, 25, 68, 85
Jessen, D. C., 12, 69, 89
Johnson, E. I., 34, 85
Johnstone, J. W. C., 26, 71, 85
Jones, C. I., 46, 86
Jones, H. L., 6, 84
Joyce, B., 34, 86

K

Kahn, R. L., 29, 69, 72, 86
Kaiser, G., 5, 31, 87
Katz, D., 29, 69, 72, 86
Kemmis, S., 6, 86
Kent, W. P., 34, 86
Kerlinger, F. N., 36, 86
Kerr, D. H., 60, 86
Kidd, J. R., 10, 28, 31, 69, 71, 72, 86, 90
Kincaid, H. V., 45, 86
Klevins, C., 33, 73, 75, 86
Klink, A. L., 9, 45, 47, 84
Knowledge, proficiency related to, 4, 46-47, 68, 74
Knowles, M. S., 3, 10, 11, 31, 33, 48, 51, 69, 72, 73, 74, 75, 86
Knox, A. B., 3, 7, 10, 11, 13, 14, 15, 19, 21, 26, 27, 28, 30, 31, 32, 33, 34, 35, 38, 39, 40, 44, 48, 51, 56, 68, 69, 70, 71, 72, 74, 75, 83, 86-87, 88
Kogan, M., 61, 87
Kotler, P., 26, 38, 71, 87
Kozoll, C. E., 28, 87
Kramer, R. E., 9, 45, 47, 84
Kreitlow, B. W., 3, 7, 24, 87
Kuusisto, E. A., 35, 89

L

Labor unions, as parent organization, 2, 10, 53, 69
Lappin, I. M., 11, 69, 80
Lauffer, A., 24, 87
Lawrence, P. R., 34, 87
Leadership, and administrators, 29-30, 71-72
Leagans, P., 5, 31, 87
Learning, by adults, 15-17, 69-70
Learning activities, 33-34, 50-51, 55, 73, 75
Legislation, related to continuing education, 62
Legislators, and policy makers, 62-63, 76
Leirman, W., 3, 5, 7, 9, 68, 92
Lemberger, A. P., 45, 80
LeTarte, C., 45, 81
Levine, H. A., 39, 87
Levinson, D. J., 15, 87
Libraries, as parent organization, 2, 53, 55
Lindquist, J., 28, 29, 65, 70, 71, 72, 87
Lippitt, G., 24, 87
Literature of field, increasing proficiency through, 10, 11-12, 14, 15, 17, 69, 70, 71
Liveright, A. A., 10, 24, 25, 68, 85
London, J., 26, 27, 71, 87
Long, H. B., 3, 87
Lorsch, J. W., 34, 87
Lowe, J., 59, 88

M

McKinley, J., 31, 88
Macy, F. V., 27, 74, 84
Madry, A. C., 3, 24, 88
Mager, R. F., 5, 33, 88
Mann, D., 60, 88
March, J. G., 19, 29, 30, 69, 72, 82
Marshall, L. E., 24, 88
Mathieson, D. E., 34, 88

Mayhew, L. B., 60, 88
Messerschmidt, D. H., 45, 88
Metcalfe, W. W., 45, 88
Mezirow, J., 19, 21, 28, 31, 69, 72, 88
Miles, M. B., 61, 88
Military, the, as parent organization, 2
Miller, D. B., 6, 88
Miller, G. A., 5, 20, 88
Miller, H. L., 33, 50, 72, 73, 75, 88
Mintzberg, H., 30, 88
Mitchell, D. E., 6, 91
Mocker, D. W., 17, 46, 47, 88
Monette, M. L., 31, 88
Moore, D. J., 45, 89
Morris, D., 50, 80
Moss, G. M., 7, 82
Mouton, J. S., 7, 29, 71, 80
Murray, N. J. M., 7, 89
Museums, as parent organization, 2

N

Nadler, L., 24, 87
Needs assessment, 31-32, 39, 47-48, 72, 74
Newell, A., 5, 20, 89
Niemi, J. A., 12, 26, 27, 35, 69, 79, 89
Niskala, H., 3, 5, 7, 9, 68, 92
Noel, J. L., 3, 5, 89

O

Objectives, setting, 33, 39, 49-50, 73, 75
Okes, I., 26, 89
Oldham, G. R., 28, 84
Orr, B., 32, 84
Osborn, A. F., 20, 89
Osterman, P., 5, 84

P

Packwood, T., 61, 87
Paisley, J., 26, 89
Palmer, R., 45, 89
Parent organizations, 2, 10-11, 60-61, 69
Parker, B., 26, 89
Parsons, J., 3, 5, 89
Participation, and administrators, 26-27, 71
Peabody, F. J., 45, 89
Penfield, K. R., 60, 89

Pennington, F., 31, 72, 89
Pepper, S., 18, 89
Performance, proficiency related to, 4
Perrone, P., 26, 89
Perspective on field, 9-17, 21, 68-69
Pipe, P., 5, 88
Pitchell, R. J., 28, 89
Policy makers: and administrators, 39; areas of proficiency for, 60-63; future proficiency of, 64-65; increasing proficiency of, 63-64; and parent organization, 65; proficiency of, 2, 18, 19, 59-66, 68; roles of, 59. *See also* Practitioners
Porter, L., 28, 89
Practitioners: and experience, 10, 11, 14, 15, 17, 69, 70; personal qualities of, 9, 17-20, 68, 70-71; perspective on the field by, 9-17, 21, 68-69; policy makers related to, 65; proficiency of, 68-71; self-directed efforts of, 7; socialization of, 9-10. *See also* Administrators; Policy makers; Resource persons
Pribram, K. H., 5, 20, 88
Price, R. K., 3, 46, 89
Process, knowledge related to, 45-46, 68, 74
Professional associations: increasing proficiency through, 10, 11, 12, 37, 69, 73; as parent organization, 2, 10, 69; and policy makers, 61, 63; workshops of, 7
Proficiency: of administrators, 2, 18-19, 34-41, 71-74; areas of, 9-22, 25-36, 45-52, 60-63; concept of, 4-6, 67; core versus specialized, 5, 68; developing, 6-8; increasing, 36-38; of policy makers, 2, 18, 19, 59-66, 68, 75-76; of resource persons, 2, 19, 43-57, 74-75; specification of, 5-6; use of, 20-22
Program administrators, 23-24, 53-54
Program development: by administrators, 23, 30-35, 68, 72-73; by resource persons, 47-52, 74-75
Program evaluation: and administrators, 34-35, 39, 73; by resource persons, 51-52, 55, 75

Q

Qazilbash, H., 3, 7, 85

R

Religious institutions, as parent organization, 2, 10, 23, 53, 69
Research: need for, 40, 56, 68, 69, 70-71, 73, 74, 75; uses of, and administration, 23, 35-36, 39, 68, 73-74
Resource persons: areas of proficiency for, 45-52; future proficiency of, 54-56; increasing proficiency of, 52-54; and learning activities, 34; mentor role of, 43, 47; need for proficiency by, 44-45; policy questions related to, 55-56; proficiency of, 2, 19, 43-57, 74-75. *See also* Practitioners
Resources: and administrators, 27-28, 32-33, 71, 72; identification of, 12-13, 69
Richman, B. M., 30, 90
Riggs, J. A., 45, 90
Rink, D. L., 45, 86
Rivera, R., 26, 71, 85
Robbins, J. N., 7, 85
Robinson, C. O., 3, 90
Rogers, J., 50, 73, 75, 90
Rose, H., 45, 90
Rosenberg, L., 34, 73, 90
Rossman, M. H., 3, 9, 90
Ruesch, J., 5, 20, 90

S

Sager, G. A., 28, 90
Sagoff, S. E., 19, 45, 90
Sanders, J. R., 34, 92
Scates, A. Y., 3, 5, 7, 90
Schein, E. H., 6, 19, 21, 28, 29, 69, 70, 90
Schneider, B., 28, 90
Schön, D. A., 19, 70, 79
Schroeder, W. L., 60, 79
Seaman, D. F., 46, 90
Self-directed study, increasing proficiency through, 37-38, 73
Sergiovanni, T. J., 28, 90
Sharma, J. C., 45, 90
Shaw, N. C., 25, 69, 71, 90
Simon, H. A., 5, 20, 89, 90
Smith, R., 50, 80
Smith, R. M., 10, 17, 18, 31, 69, 71, 72, 90
Societal influences, 11-12, 69
Solomon, D., 34, 73, 90
Sorcher, M., 28, 83

Southern Regional Education Board, 28, 91
Spady, W. G., 6, 91
Spear, G. E., 3, 5, 9, 19, 21, 28, 68, 70, 71, 91
Staff selection, 19, 28-29, 71
Stake, R. E., 6, 34, 86, 91
Stalker, G. M., 29, 81
Steele, S. M., 34, 91
Steinberg, S. S., 45, 91
Stenzel, A. K., 34, 45, 75, 91
Stufflebeam, D. L., 34, 91
Swanson, H. B., 6, 91

T

Teachers. *See* Resource persons
Thomas, A., 3, 91
Thomas, E. J., 29, 80
Thomas, H. A., 44, 92
Torshen, K. P., 6, 91
Tough, A., 3, 13, 37, 70, 91
Travers, R. M. W., 34, 91
Trivett, D. A., 6, 91
Tyler, R. W., 31, 46, 68, 92

U

Ulmer, C., 45, 92
Ussery, M. A., 46, 92

V

Vaillant, G., 15, 92
Valley, J. R., 34, 82
Van Maanen, J., 28, 92
Veri, C. C., 3, 5, 7, 9, 68, 92
Verner, C., 3, 5, 7, 9, 68, 92
Vickers, D. F., 27, 74, 84
Voluntary associations, as parent organization, 2, 10, 69
Vontress, C. E., 44, 92

W

Warren, V. B., 46, 92
Weil, M., 34, 86
Wenkert, R., 26, 27, 71, 87
Whipple, J. B., 19, 31, 92
White, R. W., 5, 92
White, T., 3, 5, 92
Wientge, K. M., 92
Williams, F. N., 43, 92

Wirt, F. M., 60, 92
Woeste, J. T., 45, 92
Wolanin, T. R., 60, 63, 83
Worthen, B. R., 34, 92

Z

Ziegler, W. L., 32, 69, 92
Zinn, L. M., 46, 92

NEW DIRECTIONS QUARTERLY SOURCEBOOKS

New Directions for Continuing Education is one of several distinct series of quarterly sourcebooks published by Jossey-Bass. The sourcebooks in each series are designed to serve both as *convenient compendiums* of the latest knowledge and practical experience on their topics and as *long-life reference tools*.

One-year, four-sourcebook subscriptions for each series cost $15 for individuals (when paid by personal check) and $25 for institutions, libraries, and agencies. Current 1979 sourcebooks are available by subscription only (however, multiple copies—five or more—are available for workshops or classroom use at $5.95 per copy).

A complete listing is given below of current sourcebooks in the *New Directions for Continuing Education* series. The titles and editors-in-chief of the other series are also listed. To subscribe, or to receive further information, write: New Directions Subscriptions, Jossey-Bass Inc., Publishers, 433 California Street, San Francisco, California 94104.

New Directions for Continuing Education
Alan B. Knox, Editor-in-Chief
1979: 1. *Enhancing Proficiencies of Continuing Educators,*
Alan B. Knox, Editor

New Directions for Child Development
William Damon, Editor-in-Chief

New Directions for Community Colleges
Arthur M. Cohen, Editor-in-Chief
Florence B. Brawer, Associate Editor

New Directions for Education and Work
Lewis C. Solmon, Editor-in-Chief

New Directions for Experiential Learning
Morris T. Keeton and Pamela J. Tate, Editors-in-Chief

New Directions for Higher Education
JB Lon Hefferlin, Editor-in-Chief

New Directions for Institutional Advancement
A. Westley Rowland, Editor-in-Chief

New Directions for Institutional Research
Marvin W. Peterson, Editor-in-Chief

New Directions for Mental Health Services
H. Richard Lamb, Editor-in-Chief

New Directions for Program Evaluation
Scarvia B. Anderson, Editor-in-Chief

New Directions for Student Services
Ursula Delworth and Gary R. Hanson, Editors-in-Chief

New Directions for Testing and Measurement
William B. Schrader, Editor-in-Chief

LC
5251
.E46

Enhancing proficiencies
of continuing educators